DEPORTATION OF THE
PRINCE EDWARD ISLAND
ACADIANS

EARLE LOCKERBY

D1158666

NIMBUS
PUBLISHING

Nimbus Publishing Limited
PO Box 9166, Halifax, NS B3K 5M8
(902) 455-4286 www.nimbus.ca

Printed and bound in Canada
NB0787
Cover and interior design: John van der Woude
Author photo: Earle Lockerby

Library and Archives Canada Cataloguing in Publication

Lockerby, Earle
Deportation of the Prince Edward Island Acadians / Earle Lockerby.
Includes bibliographical references and index. ISBN 978-1-55109-650-6
1. Acadians—Expulsion, 1758. 2. Acadians—Prince Edward Island—History. 3. Prince
Edward Island—History—To 1873. I. Title.
FC2043.5.L63 2008   971.7'004114   C2008-900822-7

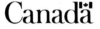

Canada Council Conseil des arts
for the Arts   du Canada

Nimbus Publishing acknowledges the financial support for its publishing activities from the
Government of Canada through the Canada Book Fund (CBF) and the Canada Council
for the Arts, and from the Province of Nova Scotia through Film & Creative Industries
Nova Scotia. We are pleased to work in partnership with Film & Creative Industries Nova
Scotia to develop and promote our creative industries for the benefit of all Nova Scotians.

To the memory of my parents, Jean and Lloyd.

Table of Contents

Foreword

ONE OF THE LESSONS HISTORIANS ARE TAUGHT WHEN THEY GO THROUGH graduate school and begin to make their way in the profession is how important it is to verify what it says in the original sources: the letters, diaries, and other documents of a given period. Those historians who went before you, the thinking goes, might have missed or, worse still, misinterpreted some telling detail in the old documents.

Earle Lockerby is definitely a historian who practices what the profession preaches regarding the need to return to the original sources. What is especially noteworthy is that Earle developed that professional discipline on his own, for he did not study history in graduate school. Rather, he is a self-taught historian. Back when he was a young man in university he chose to pursue science and engineering, and he worked for many years with a Canadian company that designs and builds nuclear power plants. It was only after he retired that Earle was able to indulge his lifelong passion for history. The end result has been numerous articles in different popular and scholarly journals, more often than not about the early history of Prince Edward Island.

Earle Lockerby's historical research and writing demonstrates over and again just how important it is to revisit what was actually written in a given time period, and not rely on handed-down interpretations. Once his curiosity is piqued Earle begins his research by reading everything written on that subject. Then he turns to the period documents, French and British alike. In the end, invariably, he comes up with insights not offered by anyone before him.

This book is the latest example of the Earle Lockerby approach. He took a subject that a number of authors have written about in a general way—the 1758 British removal of Acadians and French colonists from Île Saint-Jean (Prince Edward Island)—but for which there is no detailed analysis of all available evidence. That is exactly what Earle has done, and he has produced a study that existed nowhere previously. Because of his thoroughness and commitment to present the evidence, readers will learn in these pages more than they ever knew, or dreamed it was possible to know, about the events of 1758. Readers will be fascinated by the details of the story, and come away with a clear idea of the scale and scope of that massive population removal of 1758. This book by Earle Lockerby is one that should be widely read. It tells the story of an important, yet little-known event in Canadian history.

A. J. B. Johnston,
Historian with Parks Canada, specializing in Atlantic Canada

Acknowledgements

THE ASSISTANCE OF STAFF AT LIBRARY AND ARCHIVES CANADA, PRINCE Edward Island Archives and Records Office, Harriet Irving Library at the University of New Brunswick, Centre d'études acadiennes at the Université de Moncton, and the Robarts Library at the University of Toronto is gratefully acknowledged. I am indebted to the Parks Canada staff at the archives of Fortress Louisbourg National Historic Site for providing access to documents held there. The contribution of A. J. B. Johnston who reviewed the initial manuscript and provided the foreword to this book is much appreciated. I am grateful to Georges Arsenault for critiquing portions of the manuscript. I thank Sandra McIntyre, Caley Baker, and others at Nimbus Publishing for their expert guidance, editorial work, and other contributions that have transformed a manuscript into a finished book. Special thanks go to my wife, Heidi, for her encouragement and unwavering support.

Preface

DEPORTATION IS A DEFINING EVENT IN ACADIAN HISTORY, AND HAS PLAYED a profound role in shaping Acadian identity. For Acadians, deportation was a tragedy that resulted in the devastation of their society, the dispersal of close-knit families, and the destruction of communities. At the same time, the travails of an uprooted pastoral people during deportation and its aftermath, and the extraordinary odyssey experienced by many of them, produced a shared heritage that has helped the Acadian community re-establish itself. Acadian interpretations of deportation have provided a framework for the development of a rich, distinct, and undiminished sense of identity in the nineteenth and twentieth centuries.

Over the last two centuries historical writing about the deportation has been extensive and, like the events themselves, shaped by contesting perspectives. Most of what has been written focuses on the deportation of 1755, which resulted in the removal of approximately 6,500 Acadians from the shores of the Bay of Fundy in Nova Scotia and adjacent areas. These people were sent into exile in British colonies from Massachusetts to Georgia. Henry Wadsworth Longfellow's poem, *Evangeline: A Tale of Acadie*, played a major role in making this deportation known to Acadians and non-Acadians alike. It even imparted something of a romantic quality to the event. During the year or two following the deportation in 1755, small numbers of Acadians who had escaped deportation were apprehended and removed from Nova Scotia. In 1756, for example, about two hundred Acadians from the Cape Sable area were deported to Boston.

The second major deportation, which occurred in 1758 in Prince Edward Island (then known to the French as Île Saint-Jean), has received much less attention.˙ It is not surprising that the deportation in Nova Scotia has overshadowed the smaller, but equally traumatic and tragic one involving settlers on Île Saint-Jean three years later, as most Maritime Acadians trace their ancestry to the first deportation. This may also be attributed to the fact that the deportation from Île Saint-Jean was not the first, involved fewer people, and has been less controversial for several reasons. For one, it was carried out by a foreign country and not, as in Nova Scotia, by a country that counted the Acadians among its subjects. Moreover, unlike the deportation of 1755, the one conducted in 1758 occurred when France and Britain were officially at war.

To a large degree, however, the two deportations affected one people. Organized settlement by the French began on Île Saint-Jean in 1720; initially most settlers were from France. Over time, the population became increasingly Acadian as people moved to the Island from the mainland, particularly from 1750 to 1756. By 1758, the bulk of Île Saint-Jean's population was comprised of residents who had moved to the Island from Acadia (mainland Nova Scotia, including the isthmus of Chignecto).

˙In this book, the deportation of 1758 generally refers to the removal of people from Île Saint-Jean; however, it is important to note that concurrently, civilians and administrative and military personnel were removed from Île Royale (Cape Breton).

Although a great deal has been published about the deportation of 1755, it attracted little historical attention during the first century after the event. In the second half of the nineteenth century and early part of the twentieth, as historical interest in the subject grew, writers tended to treat the subject as a matter for debate. Just as the deportation involved English-speaking Protestants on the one hand and French-speaking Catholics on the other, the writing in this period also reflected defensive and accusatory postures, depending upon the author's religious or ethnic background. As the twentieth century concluded, historical writing related to Acadian deportation became less partisan, though in the case of Île Saint-Jean, it was not necessarily characterized by greater accuracy.

Catholic clerics did much of the early writing about the deportations of 1755 and 1758. This began in France in 1766 with Abbé Guillaume-Thomas-François Raynal's attack on British tyranny for the deportation of Acadians, and continued in Canada with Henri-Raymond Casgrain's late-nineteenth-century works concerning the deportations. Casgrain's interpretation of the deportation from Île Saint-Jean was reinforced early in the twentieth century by John C. MacMillan, and again, by J. Wilfred Pineau, well beyond the midpoint of the century. Both were priests from Prince Edward Island.

In recent decades most of what has been written on the deportations has emerged as part of larger works on the history of the Acadians. The 1758 deportation from Île Saint-Jean has been addressed in works concerning Acadians in general or Acadians of Prince Edward Island, and in histories of Prince Edward Island and of the Catholic Church on the Island. Within these frameworks, the expulsion of Île Saint-Jean's inhabitants has rarely been the subject of more than a few pages, and more commonly of only a few sentences or paragraphs. Surprisingly, little or no research on the deportation appeared during the seventy years prior to the time that the research for this book was undertaken.

Most of what is known about the deportation of Île Saint-Jean's settlers is based on official records in archives in London. Relatively little information is available from archives in France or Québec. Indeed, little about the deportation found its way into official French-language records of the time. This book relies more heavily upon British records than French records simply because, as they relate to the deportation of 1758, the former are considerably more plentiful than the latter. The relative paucity of French records should not be surprising. French officials and the Acadians, who were defeated and in great disarray, were not inclined to write about their circumstances, whether they were military officers, administrative personnel, or ordinary inhabitants, of whom few could in fact write. On the other hand, British officers were managing the deportation operations. This entailed issuing written instructions, keeping logs, and advising superiors by letter of events in the field.

There is, however, a great deal of information in French archives concerning assistance to approximately 1,500 refugees from Île Saint-Jean who found themselves in France. This information is frequently inextricably grouped with similar information for refugees from Île Royale, as the French called Cape Breton.

Two or three of the historians who have written about the deportation from Île Saint-Jean have relied on primary sources (documents dating from the event itself or shortly thereafter). The vast majority appears to have relied largely on secondary sources—they have echoed the writings of earlier historians. Writing that relies on secondary sources often becomes the authority for subsequent works, an iterative process that compounds and entrenches inaccuracies and misinformation.

The fact that little new primary research on the deportation has appeared in many decades might suggest that archival records are sparse, and have already been used to their fullest. This is not true. Records in British archives that have received insufficient attention can provide a better understanding of the logistics of the deportation operation, and the fate of the shiploads of deportees. Admiralty records are particularly important in this regard, as they include: the log of the *Hind*, the warship used by

Lieutenant-Colonel Rollo for transportation to and from Île Saint-Jean, and for convoying the transports (or vessels) used to evacuate the inhabitants; Admiral Boscawen's journal, which identifies the transports used in the deportation; documents which provide further information about these vessels, and the identities of their masters; and documents concerning passengers on transports that stopped at English ports. War Office records, including correspondence from officials in Louisbourg to authorities in London, shed additional light on the deportation.

Archives in France hold documents concerning the arrival of the transports in French ports, which help us to gain a better understanding of the deportation. Perhaps the most useful data from French archives are lists of inhabitants from Île Saint-Jean who debarked from seven transports at Saint-Malo, as well as the names of people on these vessels who died en route. These lists were copied, translated, and edited a quarter century ago by two individuals from Louisiana. The existence of these records, drawn from the archives of the Port of Saint-Servan, has not been widely known, and they have been little used in studies concerning the deportation of 1758. This book draws from new sources such as these to provide a more comprehensive view of the deportation operation than has previously been published. It also addresses several commonly held misconceptions concerning the deportation of French settlers from Île Saint-Jean.

Chapter 1

Evolution of Île Saint-Jean
to 1758

THE CANADIAN PROVINCE NOW KNOWN AS PRINCE EDWARD ISLAND was once a territory of France called Île Saint-Jean. By the Treaty of Utrecht (1713) this island (then inhabited only by the Mi'kmaq) and Île Royale were retained by France, while Acadia was ceded to Britain. Organized settlement began in 1720 under the auspices of Louis-Charles Hyacinthe Castel, better known as the Comte de Saint-Pierre. In the previous year he had been granted all of the Island by the French Crown on the condition that he colonize it in return for fishing rights. The company he founded to pursue the fishery collapsed after a few years. Nevertheless, the Comte de Saint-Pierre succeeded in laying the foundation for a sedentary (shore-based) fishery, a growing colony, and what would eventually become a haven to a significant fraction of the overall Acadian population. Though the colony of Île Saint-Jean, which was a dependency of Île Royale, had a fairly brief existence—from 1720 to

1758—it figures prominently in the eighteenth-century history of the Acadian people.

Early years on the Island

Almost all the original settlers on Île Saint-Jean came directly from France and established themselves at Port-la-Joie and Havre Saint-Pierre (St. Peter's Harbour). However, during the first year of the colony a few Acadians began to migrate to Île Saint-Jean from Nova Scotia. One of the earliest and most prominent Acadians to relocate was Michel Haché-Gallant who came from Beaubassin with his wife, Anne Cormier. They settled permanently at Port-la-Joie. During the two decades following the failure of the Comte de Saint-Pierre's company, Acadian migration continued

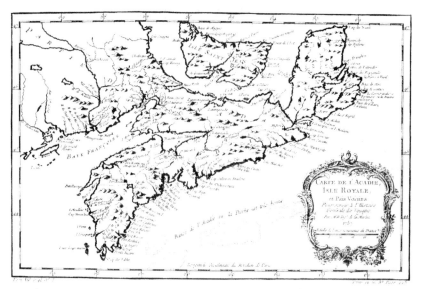

French cartographer Jacques-Nicolas Bellin's map of 1757 shows Île Saint-Jean, Île Royale, and Acadia.

slowly but fairly steadily, gradually changing the Island's complexion from French to Acadian. New settlements were established along the Rivière-du-Nord-Est (Hillsborough River) and at Malpec. Havre Saint-Pierre was soon the most populous district, and it retained this distinction throughout the remainder of the French regime on the Island. It was also the main base for the fishery.

This monument to Michel Haché-Gallant and his wife, Anne Cormier, stands at Port-la-Joye–Fort Amherst National Historic Site.

Beginning in 1749, at a time when the Island's population was only about 735, France put renewed and increased emphasis on its policy of encouraging Acadians to relocate from British territory to French territory, namely Île Royale and Île Saint-Jean. Incentives, such as free passage for themselves, their household effects, baggage, and livestock were offered, as well as implements and food for one year. These incentives, combined with anxiety about political and military developments in Nova Scotia, including disagreements over the boundary of Acadia, led to a much greater rate of inflow of Acadians to Île Saint-Jean than had been previously experienced. New settlements were begun at Pointe-Prime, Bedec, and other places, and older settlements grew quickly.

From the colony's earliest years a small administrative unit and a garrison were maintained at Port-la-Joie, detached from Louisbourg, the seat of government for both Île Royale and Île Saint-Jean. Usually less than one hundred soldiers were stationed at the garrison. It was Louisbourg,

Depiction of the fortified town of Louisbourg, which was the seat of power for Île Royale and its dependency, Île Saint-Jean.

however, that implemented policy and furnished support of various kinds. As the colony grew, fishing continued at Havre Saint-Pierre, but agriculture became the predominant endeavour of the inhabitants. Cattle, sheep, pigs, and chickens were the most common livestock, but some settlers also raised geese and turkeys. Wheat was the principal crop, though some oats and peas were grown. The most common beasts of burden were oxen, followed by horses. Interestingly, potatoes were not grown. Authorities at Louisbourg promoted farming on the Island as a means of providing foodstuffs to Louisbourg and its large garrison. They anticipated that Île Saint-Jean would become the breadbasket for Île Royale, which had less favourable soil and climate. To encourage agriculture, fishing was strongly discouraged by the king, and therefore was also discouraged by Louisbourg, except at Havre Saint-Pierre.

Acadian farmers along the shore of the Bay of Fundy were used to traditional marshland farming, employing dikes to hold back the sea. In Île

Saint-Jean there was less marshland and the tides were much
lower. There the Acadians did
seek out marshland, but only
used dikes occasionally. They
pursued some upland agriculture involving tree clearing. Île
Saint-Jean experienced more
than its share of infestations
of mice and grasshoppers,
which devoured crops in the
fields. Occasionally, forest fires
spread to the farms, destroying
not only crops, but homes and
farm buildings as well. Not
infrequently there were serious
food shortages and even famine. Sometimes settlers had no
choice but to eat the grain that

French soldiers of the Compagnies Franches de la Marine were deployed at Port-la-Joie.

had been reserved for planting the following spring. Louisbourg did its
best to alleviate these problems, but often fell short.

Increased population, greater challenges

The strong commercial and administrative links with Louisbourg were
increasingly supplemented by strong family connections between the
settlers of Île Saint-Jean and their kinfolk in Nova Scotia at places
such as Beaubassin, Cobequid, Grand-Pré, and Pisiquid. The Island's
population became an increasingly integral part of the overall Acadian
community. The policy of Acadian relocation was so successful that from

Acadian farmers on Île Saint-Jean utilized marshland as well as upland.

1749 to the summer of 1755 the Island's population quadrupled to about three thousand. Acadians embarking at such places on the mainland as Tatamagouche, Cocagne, and Baie Verte continued to make their way across the Mer Rouge (Northumberland Strait). A surge in the number of new arrivals occurred during the months following the fall of Fort Beauséjour to British and New England soldiers in 1755. It was there, in the Chignecto region, that the deportation of 1755 began, and a large number of Acadians from this area eluded their would-be captors by escaping to Île Saint-Jean.

The influx of Acadians to Île Saint-Jean during the 1750s put an enormous strain on the colony. Despite good intentions, Louisbourg failed miserably in adequately providing the new arrivals with basic necessities. Food shortages became endemic, and occasionally new settlers were close to starvation. Rarely were there two or three good harvests in succession. Even clothing was in short supply. In the fall of 1753 Abbé Jacques Girard at Pointe-Prime wrote: "Our refugees do not lose courage and hope by working to be able to live; but the nakedness which is almost universal and extreme affects them sorely. I assure you they cannot protect themselves from cold, either by day or night. Most of the children are so naked they cannot cover themselves…All are not reduced to this extremity, but almost all are in great need." The impact on the settlers who had established themselves prior to 1749, many of whom had family ties with the new arrivals, was immense.

Matters did not improve over the next few years. In 1756 some inhabitants were sent to Québec as a relief measure. A few crossed to Miramichi in an effort to find better living conditions. They found conditions at refugee camps in Miramichi housing Acadians who had fled from Nova Scotia in 1755 and 1756 to be truly appalling. On the eve of the 1758 deportation there were slightly fewer than five thousand inhabitants on Île Saint-Jean, mostly Acadians. The inhabitants were distributed largely from Malpec in the west to the eastern tip of the Island, in a number of discrete

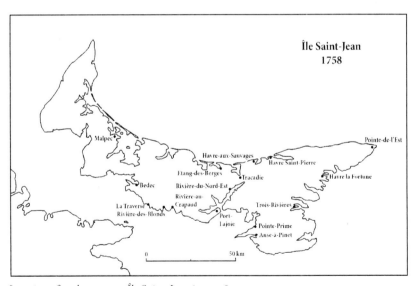

Location of settlements on Île Saint-Jean in 1758

communities comprising five parishes. The bulk of the population lived on the eastern half of the Island.

While conditions in Acadia just before the cataclysm of 1755 were less idyllic than those depicted in Longfellow's *Evangeline*, conditions in Île Saint-Jean just prior to the catastrophe of 1758 were exceedingly difficult. As the summer of 1758 unfolded, the hope that the Acadian refugees possessed, referred to above by Abbé Girard, was soon to be shattered.

Chapter 2

End of the French Colonial Regime

THE BRITISH MILITARY CAMPAIGN AGAINST FRANCE FOR CONTROL of eastern North America called for attacks on both Québec and Louisbourg in 1757. When delays forced one of these objectives to be dropped, Louisbourg became the lone target, but because British military commanders perceived French land and naval forces at Louisbourg to be overwhelming, they decided to forego even this more limited prize. However, the following year British Secretary of State William Pitt resolved to take Louisbourg, and committed the resources to succeed. The expedition against Louisbourg was commanded by Major General Jeffery Amherst and included Brigadier James Wolfe, who one year later would be the hero of the Plains of Abraham at Québec. The siege of Louisbourg by both land and sea forces lasted for seven weeks.

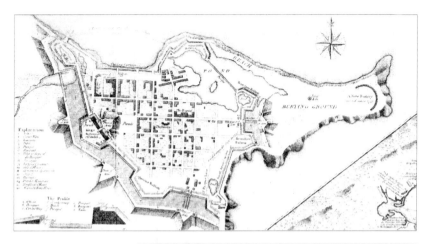

(above) The fortress of Louisbourg was built to enable the French to dominate the lucrative fishery in the northwestern Atlantic, and to guard the entrance to the Gulf of St. Lawrence. It was intended to provide some protection to France's most important North American colony, Canada.

(right) Jeffery Amherst (1717–97), commander-in-chief in the American theatre from 1758 to 1763, directed the siege of Louisbourg in the summer of 1758.

In the foreground British soldiers construct a siege battery from which to bombard the fortress at Louisbourg (centre) and French warships (right).

The fate of Île Saint-Jean's residents was sealed on July 26, 1758, the day that Governor Augustin de Boschenry de Drucour surrendered Louisbourg, the seat of government for both Île Royale and its dependency, Île Saint-Jean. Although the articles of capitulation provided for the removal of the French garrison on Île Saint-Jean, none of the articles addressed the fate of ordinary civilians in either Île Royale or Île Saint-Jean. However, within days of the capitulation it became clear that British policy was to deport all inhabitants, civilian as well as military, from both places. The fall of the fortress of Louisbourg marked the end of the French regime in Atlantic Canada and doomed the residents of Île Saint-Jean to deportation and forfeit of their homes and lands.

British forces take control

The man Amherst chose to arrange for the capitulation of Île Saint-Jean, the removal of its inhabitants, and the construction of a fort at Port-la-Joie was fifty-eight-year-old Lieutenant-Colonel Andrew Rollo. Prior to

Lieutenant-Colonel Andrew Rollo (1703–1765) was selected by Amherst to carry out the deportation of Île Saint-Jean's inhabitants.

the siege of Louisbourg, Rollo had distinguished himself at Dettingen, Bavaria, and seen action at Albany and Schenectady in New York. Amherst's instructions to Rollo were issued at Louisbourg on August 8, 1758. Rollo was to proceed immediately to Île Saint-Jean with 500 men in four transport vessels— the *King of Prussia* with 140 troops, the *Dunbar* with 140 troops, the *Bristol* with 130 troops, and the *Catherine* with 90 troops. The troops included 300 infantry drawn from the regiments of Whitmore, Bragg, Warburton, and Hopson, as well as 200 light infantry and rangers. The transport vessels, victualled for three months, were convoyed by the twenty-four-gun man-of-war *Hind*, whose master was Robert Bond. The transports also carried one thousand palisades, boards, spikes, nails, and tools to be used by 300 men to construct a redoubt, or fort, at Port-la-Joie.

Drucour, the defeated French governor, was to send along two or three of his officers from Louisbourg to inform the garrison and inhabitants on Île Saint-Jean of the articles of capitulation, including the requirement that they surrender themselves and their firearms. All inhabitants who surrendered or were taken alive were to be brought to Louisbourg on the four transports as soon as the fort was completed, along with the British military personnel who were not being left at Port-la-Joie to man the fort.

Though the fort on the hill at left (shown in this sketch of Port-la-Joie from 1734) was never constructed, the settlement did have more modest fortifications.

If the number of prisoners made this impossible the transports were to remove all of the inhabitants to Louisbourg immediately, and then return to Port-la-Joie to pick up the troops. A British garrison of about one hundred men was to be left at Port-la-Joie. Their task was to man the newly constructed fort, which came to be known as Fort Amherst.

Rollo lost little time in carrying out his assigned duties. The *Hind*, with the four transports and a schooner, cleared Louisbourg on August 10 and sailed through the Strait of Canso on August 13. The *Hind's* log shows that at 2:00 PM on August 17, as it was approaching the harbour at Port-la-Joie, a boat bearing a flag of truce came out to meet it. Captain Bond sent his cutter to intercept the boat. At 3:00 PM the *Hind* "fired a gun and the [French] Fort was surrendered." The surrender was by the Island's major and commandant, Gabriel Rousseau de Villejouin. The day ended with the British vessels moored in the harbour, and with the capitulation having been extended to Île Saint-Jean.

By the time the *Hind* left Louisbourg, if not before, Villejouin was aware that the British would soon be coming to Île Saint-Jean to remove him and his garrison. However, he was expecting only a packet boat (*paquebot*) for the removal of the garrison. Evidently, at that time he did not know the full extent of Rollo's evacuation plans. It is unlikely however that the population was caught totally unawares, and in all probability they had taken some precautions. Louisbourg had been under threat for two or

Chart of the harbour at Port-la-Joie in 1754. The garrison and main concentration of homes were situated on the west side of the narrows, which led to the estuaries of three rivers.

three years, and the inhabitants of Île Saint-Jean had known for some time that their situation was precarious. In the summer of 1756 Villejouin issued arms to some civilians, and had some stores moved up the Rivière-du-Nord-Est (later named the Hillsborough River) from Port-la-Joie. He had also advised farmers to conceal their families and livestock in the woods as a drill to enhance their awareness of the need for defensive tactics, and to improve their ability to implement them if required.

Chapter 3

Commencement of Arrests

THE FRENCH GARRISON AND ADMINISTRATIVE OFFICIALS WERE AMONG the first people taken into custody on Île Saint-Jean. To ensure that the deportation operation could proceed without major difficulty, it was necessary to neutralize these individuals. The speedy capture and incarceration of French soldiers and officials sent a strong signal to the inhabitants that they should surrender without resistance. Rollo's forces took advantage of "moderate and fair" weather on August 18 to go up the Rivière-du-Nord-Est "to bring down some French Prisoners." The *Hind's* log shows that on the following day at 3:00 PM, Rollo's men "brought down the French Prisoners and three 6 Pounders." It is likely that these three cannons had been installed by the French on the north side of the Hillsborough River, slightly downstream of an island known today as Rams Island (formerly known as McNally's Island) near present-day

Admiral Edward Boscawen (1711–61), commander of naval forces, arranged for transports to be sent to Île Saint-Jean for deportation of the Acadians and ordered their masters to proceed to Port-la-Joie.

Frenchfort. During the following week, the transports discharged their supplies, and the *Hind* received on-board ten steers and nineteen sheep "for the use of the Ship's Company."

On August 24 the British sighted two French schooners coming down the river, and they were followed two days later by a schooner loaded with prisoners from the head of the river. British forces continued to round up inhabitants and place them on the transports until August 31 when the convoy, with 692 passengers, weighed anchor and headed for Louisbourg Harbour. It arrived on September 4, bringing a letter from Rollo that indicated that most of the inhabitants had "brought in their arms & [would] embark for Europe." The journal of Admiral Edward Boscawen, who commanded the naval forces that blockaded and bombarded Louisbourg in 1758, notes that "five transports" in convoy with the *Hind* arrived in Louisbourg with prisoners from Île Saint-Jean. This is one ship more than the fleet originally assigned to Rollo. The additional transport may have been the schooner Rollo brought with him to Île Saint-Jean, or one of the French schooners found there.

Deportation underway: Villejouin's perspective

One of the few contemporary French documents describing the deportation on Île Saint-Jean is a letter dated September 8, 1758, written by Villejouin while aboard a vessel in the harbour of Port-la-Joie. In the letter, which is addressed to the minister in France responsible for colonies, Villejouin indicates that some of the settlers on Île Saint-Jean had gone to an Acadian refugee camp in the Miramichi area to evade deportation. Unknown to the British (at least until 1758), this camp existed from 1756 to 1759, and sheltered Acadians who had eluded capture by British soldiers. Misery in the camp was immense, and it has been estimated that well over a thousand people died there from starvation and disease. Not surprisingly, those who went there from Île Saint-Jean, hoping to better their situation, chose to return and to face deportation.

According to Villejouin, Rollo permitted two priests from Île Saint-Jean, Pierre Cassiet and Jean Biscarat, to travel to Louisbourg with a petition from the inhabitants of the Island, requesting that they be allowed to remain on their lands. British authorities at Louisbourg denied the request. Villejouin also reported that seven hundred settlers had been made to embark when he had, and that they were still in the harbour of Port-la-Joie. He estimated that four thousand settlers remained to be deported, and expressed doubt that Rollo would succeed in taking them all that year. He also estimated that there were more than six thousand cattle on the Island, the same number reported about a year earlier by Governor Vaudreuil of Québec.

The information provided by Villejouin raises questions. On what vessels were Villejouin and close to 700 others being held on September 8? The transports that had come to Port-la-Joie with Rollo sailed for Louisbourg on August 31, arriving there with their loads of prisoners on September 4. Additional transports are not known to have reached Port-la-Joie until early October. One possibility is that Villejouin and the settlers were detained on schooners taken from the French on Île Saint-Jean. A more likely explanation is that the 700 detainees referred to by Villejouin were actually the 692 prisoners sent to Louisbourg on transports on August 31. In this case, is the date of Villejouin's letter incorrect, or was the date inserted at Louisbourg some days after Villejouin had started the letter? The garrison and government officials, including Villejouin, would almost certainly have been taken to Louisbourg aboard the first available vessels.

The first to depart for Europe

Villejouin wrote that he expected his family to be travelling to Rochefort in France. The plan was to ship non-combatant prisoners of war, such as the French and Acadian settlers, to France. Villejouin and his colleagues from Port-la-Joie, as well as all of the military personnel at Louisbourg, were considered combatant prisoners of war. Consequently, they were destined to be shipped to England and detained there for some time. Villejouin proceeded to Louisbourg where Boscawen placed him, along with nineteen military officers from Louisbourg and twenty-four others, aboard the warship *York* under the command of Hugh Pigot. After a difficult passage begun on September 13, the *York* reached Spithead (near Portsmouth), England, around October 27.

The French soldiers of the garrison at Port-la-Joie, numbering less than one hundred, were shipped from Louisbourg to England, as were roughly three thousand soldiers comprising the garrisons of Louisbourg and other military posts on Île Royale. While some of the military prisoners may have been detained in England, perhaps until the close of the Seven Years' War in 1763, many were transferred to France during the fall of 1758 and the first half of 1759.

The civilian prisoners delivered to Louisbourg in early September 1758 were sent to France soon after on other vessels. In Boscawen's journal, immediately after the entry concerning the arrival of the *Hind* and its convoy

This painting depicts the harbour at Port-la-Joie where British soldiers embarked approximately two-thirds of Île Saint-Jean's inhabitants on ships destined for France.

on September 4, an entry states that he had "Order'd Thomas Hurry, Ma[s] of the Duke of Cumberland Transp[t], to receive 327 Fr. Prisoners & carry them to Rochelle, there to receive 38 English Prisoners in exchange and carry them to Plymouth." Similarly, on September 10 the *Richmond* and *Britannia* were dispatched from Louisbourg to La Rochelle with 284 and 312 prisoners respectively. At La Rochelle they would pick up 248 English prisoners and convey them to Plymouth. A little over two weeks later, two transports, the *Sukey* and *Mary*, left Louisbourg for Saint-Malo with more than 600 prisoners. These were just a few of the transports sent off from Louisbourg loaded with prisoners. Most carried people who had been living in Louisbourg and Île Royale. The *Mary*, however, was loaded with prisoners from Île Saint-Jean.

Chapter 4

The Operation Expands

BRITISH AUTHORITIES GROSSLY UNDERESTIMATED THE NUMBER OF people living on Île Saint-Jean. Boscawen acknowledged that the British had estimated the total population was only four or five hundred. Once Rollo provided his superiors at Louisbourg with revised estimates, they recognized they would need many more transports and quickly obtained them. Admiral Boscawen wrote on September 8 that he "order'd 13 Transports to be supplied with two months provisions from the Commissary of Stores, for 3540 French Prisoners to be received on board them at the Isle St Johns." Three days later he wrote that he had directed Charles Hay, agent for the transports, to proceed under convoy of the *Hind* to Île Saint-Jean with fourteen transports (see Table 1) to take on board all the prisoners. They would then proceed to Saint-Malo, France. At Saint-Malo, they would exchange the French prisoners from Île Saint-Jean for English prisoners, and convey the English prisoners to the River Thames.

On September 8, 1758, Boscawen wrote in his journal that he ordered provisions for two months to be put aboard the transports that would carry 3,540 deportees from Île Saint-Jean.

TABLE 1 Transports Used in Île Saint-Jean Deportation (identified on September 11, 1758)

Name of vessel	Master	Burden, or Carrying Capacity (tons)	Guns
Briton	James Wilson	343	8
Duke William	William Nichols	400	10
John & Samuel	William Dobson	239	6
Mathias	Thomas Dobbins	193	6
Neptune	John Beaton	234	6
Parnassus	William Johnson	425	7
Patience	Daniel Stephens	183	6
Restoration	Stephenson Haxton	177	6
Ruby	William Kelly	380	6
Supply	William Wallace	189	3
Tamerlane	Charles Suttie	215	6
Three Sisters	Christopher Douson	247	6
Violet	Benjamin Suggitt	315	7
Yarmouth	Samuel Henry	375	8

Preparations and provisions

While the transports were being provisioned at Louisbourg, the *Hind* also took on new supplies, including fifteen firkins (614 litres) of butter, fifty hundredweight (2,273 kilograms) of bread, and six puncheons (1,909 litres) of beer. On September 14 the *Hind* set out once more from Louisbourg for Île Saint-Jean, this time with the fourteen transports plus a schooner and another vessel. Due to unfavourable weather, the large number of vessels, and the nature of the route (the narrow Strait of Canso), Captain Bond had difficulty advancing to Île Saint-Jean and keeping the convoy together. By September 26 the *Hind* was about ten kilometres southeast of Pictou Island, and was off Île Saint-Jean's East Point by the

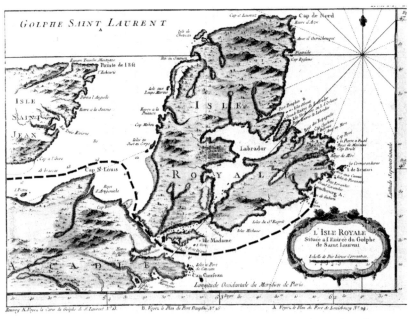

The route taken by the transports from Louisbourg to Port-la-Joie (depicted on this map by French cartographer Bellin) included the difficult passage through the narrow Strait of Canso.

following day. There the *Yarmouth* grounded. Other transports assisted in refloating the vessel the next day and it was able to continue. By September 29, however, squalls had pushed the *Hind* back into Saint Georges Bay, a few leagues from the northwestern end of the Strait of Canso.

While the *Hind* struggled to deliver its charges to Port-la-Joie, authorities in Louisbourg had decided that additional vessels were required at Île Saint-Jean. On September 18 Boscawen's journal notes that he "order'd the masters of the Transports *Richard and Mary, Scarborough* and *Mary* to proceed to Saint Johns, & there place themselves under the Command of Capt. Bond of the *Hind*, & Mr. Chas Hay Agent for Transports" (see Table 2). Nothing further is known about the movement of the three additional vessels that Boscawen ordered to Île Saint-Jean. However, the *Hind's* log indicates that on September 24 "his Majesty's ships *Juno* and *Etna* with sev^l Transports" passed through the Strait of Canso. On the following day a sloop and a ship came through the strait as well. The three additional vessels ordered to Île Saint-Jean by Boscawen almost certainly made the trip since one, the *Richard and Mary*, is known to have run into problems after leaving Port-la-Joie.

By October 3 Captain Bond finally succeeded in getting his convoy into the harbour of Port-la-Joie. The next day Bond sent a sloop up the

TABLE 2 Transports Added to Deportation Operation on September 18, 1758)

Name of vessel	Master	Burden, or Carrying Capacity (tons)	Guns
Richard & Mary	John Moore	252	5
Scarborough	Jonathon Fellour	95	0
Mary	Three small- to medium-sized transports named *Mary* were used in the Louisbourg expedition. They ranged in size from 92 to 222 tons. It is unclear which of the three was ordered to proceed to Île Saint-Jean.		

Rivière-du-Nord-Est with a petty officer and six men to retrieve cattle. Four men were assigned the same task on October 6. In addition to obtaining beef, the first week and a half at Port-la-Joie was spent loading provisions onto the transports, including "wooding the ships" (presumably bringing on board supplies of firewood). Provisioning continued off and on throughout the time that the vessels were at Port-la-Joie. Crew brought water aboard the vessels on a number of occasions, and one day, members of the *Hind*'s crew were sent ashore to brew spruce beer. On October 14 a schooner arrived at Port-la-Joie from Pointe-Prime carrying fifty French inhabitants. On October 15 Captain Bond sent longboats from the *Hind* up the river to receive additional inhabitants. The British continued to round up settlers until about the beginning of November.

Evading the roundup

Not all of Île Saint-Jean's residents submitted to British orders to turn themselves in. Rollo informed Boscawen, in a letter dated October 10, that "numbers have fled to Canada and carried off great quantities of cattle by means of 4 Schooners which ply from Magpeck [Malpec] to ye Continent." A letter dated October 12 from Captain Bond acknowledged the difficulty that the troops were having in getting the inhabitants to submit. He mentioned that a French or Acadian armed schooner mounting six guns was assisting the Acadians to evade the British roundup by fleeing to the mainland.

Two days after Bond wrote this letter it was in the hands of Rear-Admiral Philip Durell, Boscawen's successor at Louisbourg. Durell believed the armed schooner to be one that Captain Vaughan and Brigadier James Murray had chased into the harbour at Miramichi during a raiding foray there on or about September 15. On receiving this information from Île Saint-Jean, Durell ordered Captain Maximillian Jacobs to proceed from

In his log, Rear-Admiral Philip Durell recorded the news that an armed vessel and some schooners, owned and operated by the Acadians, on the north shore were helping fugitives flee to the mainland.

Louisbourg with the armed cruiser *Kennington* "with the utmost dispatch on a Cruize to the Northward of the Island of Saint Johns, and use his utmost endeavour to destroy the said armed French Ship and Schooners, and after being upon that Station some days, to proceed to the entrance of the River Saint Lawrence."

On October 18 Durell dispatched a sloop to Île Saint-Jean to advise Rollo of the action he was taking. Having been provided with a pilot familiar with the Island, the *Kennington* set out on October 20. The *Kennington*, which was to cruise off the north shore of the Island for eight or ten days, encountered nothing of significance. This is hardly surprising, since after passing through Cabot Strait, it followed a course that took it well to the north of the Magdalen Islands and on to Gaspé. This route kept it distant from Île Saint-Jean.

Among those helping settlers escape from the north shore of Île Saint-Jean was Nicolas Gautier, who came from a prominent family in Acadia noted for its opposition to British rule. According to one Acadian historian, Nicolas's father was one of the most important people in Acadia in

e. Nicolas, his father, and other family members had moved from dia to Île Saint-Jean about 1749. Shortly before the fall of Louisbourg 1758, he relocated to the head of the Bay of Chaleur. Under the auspices of Jean-Francois Bourdon, the commander at Restigouche, and Charles Deschamps de Boishébert, a Canadian soldier who pursued guerrilla activities in Acadia from 1746 to 1749 and from 1754 to 1758, Gautier almost certainly employed one or more schooners during the summer and fall of 1758 to help settlers on the north side of Île Saint-Jean escape to Miramichi and the Bay of Chaleur region. His rescue operation was no doubt an integral part of the evasive activities reported in October by Rollo and Bond. A few inhabitants may have fled to Saint-Pierre et Miquelon as well.

As the end of October approached, British efforts to take in prisoners drew to a close. In a letter, Reverend Jacques Girard, the parish priest at Pointe-Prime, writes that he and "a fair number of inhabitants from my parish" were embarked at Port-la-Joie on October 20. The embarkment of Girard and at least some members of the parish of Pointe-Prime occurred toward the end of the period during which the inhabitants of Île Saint-Jean were uprooted. Girard was embarked on the *Duke William*, one of the largest transports brought to Port-la-Joie. According to one account, he conducted many marriages during the weeks before the transports left Port-la-Joie, as the deportees believed that single men deported to France would be forced to become soldiers, a fate they wished to avoid.

Left behind

On October 30 the master of a sloop that had arrived at Louisbourg reported that 1,600 of Île Saint-Jean's inhabitants had been embarked, and that the approximately 600 remaining settlers would have to stay for the winter. A letter from Rollo to Governor Whitmore at Louisbourg confirmed those numbers, and reported that the troops at Port-la-Joie were to embark

Inhabitants, old and young, dejectedly contemplate their fate as British soldiers give instructions.

for Louisbourg on October 28. In a letter to Boscawen, dated November 5, Durell noted that the settlers who would remain in Port-la-Joie were "sickly and most of them Women and Children." Shipboard epidemics due to contagious disease were a major concern; however, except for the inhabitants of the Malpec area, for which the British soldiers could not spare the time and resources to apprehend, very few inhabitants were left behind.

In a letter to an Admiralty official in London, also dated November 5, Durell reported receiving correspondence from Bond indicating that two thousand inhabitants had been deported on sixteen transports (all that Bond had). The transports were sent to France as cartel ships, meaning that they sailed under a flag of truce. Agents of Britain and France had mutually agreed that such vessels were not to be seized or interfered with while carrying out their mission of prisoner exchange.

A day later, Governor Whitmore wrote British Secretary of State William Pitt, to tell him of the latest news from Rollo. Rollo had written that about 2,200 inhabitants of Île Saint-Jean had been embarked. In addition, Whitmore advised Pitt that despite this achievement, Rollo had also informed him that "much against his Inclinations He is obliged to leave the Inhabitants of a whole Parish behind. They live at a distant part of the Island about a hundred Miles by land which is Impracticable for Them to March and the Agent for the Transports (one Capt Hay) told my Lord Rollo and Capt Bond of His Majesty's Ship *Hinde* He would protest against it if They were. Admiral Durel has Sent further Orders since this Advice and I hope They will be Embarked." This parish was La Sainte-Famille located at Malpec in the vicinity of the present-day Port Hill.

"Ship'd off"

In a letter dated November 11 Whitmore provided Amherst with more precise and up-to-date figures. A sloop he had sent to Île Saint-Jean on October 19 returned on November 5 with a letter from Rollo (dated October 28) indicating that 2,150 of the inhabitants had been "ship'd off." This number was apparently in addition to the 692 Rollo said were aboard the transports that the *Hind* had taken into Louisbourg Harbour on September 4. Yet a further revision of the numbers embarked is made in a letter of November 21 from Whitmore to Amherst in which he says: "By the Returns I have recd from the Island of Saint Johns, Two Thousand four hundred & fifteen persons were Embark'd for France." This number was confirmed by Charles Hay, agent for the transports, upon his subsequent arrival in England. Presumably, this figure also does not include the 692 taken to Louisbourg in September.

A few inhabitants of Île Saint-Jean experienced double tragedy, as their removal by Rollo's forces was their second deportation. The Island's population included a handful of settlers who had been deported from the mainland to the Carolinas in 1755, and who had since made their way to

Île Saint-Jean. For many Acadians, the deportation of 1758 represented the beginning of an odyssey that would take them to such scattered places as France, Saint-Pierre et Miquelon, islands in the Caribbean, Guiana, Corsica, Louisiana, and even the Falkland Islands. Inhabitants of Île Saint-Jean ended up in all or most of these places, though in many instances they stayed for only a few years.

Chapter 5

Beginning of a Transatlantic Odyssey

O N NOVEMBER 4 AT 7:00 AM UNDER FAIR SKIES AND IN MODER-
ATE winds the *Hind* and the vessels under its charge unmoored
and set sail, leaving the harbour of Port-la-Joie behind. The convoy led by
the *Hind* included the transports *Briton, Duke William, John and Samuel,
Mathias, Neptune, Parnassus, Patience, Restoration, Richard and Mary, Ruby,
Supply, Tamerlane, Three Sisters, Violet,* and *Yarmouth.* The *Briton* and the
Richard and Mary carried troops no longer required at Port-la-Joie or Fort
Amherst—along with the *Hind,* they were destined for Louisbourg. The
other ships were destined for France.

By November 5 they reached the entrance to the Strait of Canso. The
following afternoon squalls developed, and the *Tamerlane* was driven
ashore in the strait. The next day strong gales also sent the *Parnassus* ashore,
and the *Hind's* cutter sought to assist it. On November 13 the *Richard
and Mary* struck a submerged rock off Île Madame. It displayed a distress

A convoy of ships, most of them bound for France, leaves Port-la-Joie. Three did not make it safely across the Atlantic Ocean.

signal, and subsequently ran in for the shore of Île Madame. The *Hind* attempted to approach the transport in order to assist it, but failed because of an ebb tide. The *Hind* and *Briton* continued to Louisbourg, arriving there on November 14.

The British refloated the *Tamerlane*, but abandoned the stranded *Parnassus* as a wreck. They placed its passengers, all of whom were saved, aboard one or more of the other transports. As for the *Richard and Mary*, authorities sent help as soon as the *Hind* reached Louisbourg. Whitmore readied two sloops or schooners to assist the *Richard and Mary*, but contrary winds delayed their departure until November 20. In the meantime, Whitmore sent an officer and twenty Rangers overland along the coast to obtain what intelligence they could about the stricken vessel. Whitmore received word by land during the morning of November 22 that although the *Richard and Mary* had sunk very quickly after striking the rock, all of the passengers had gotten off safely. John Moore, master of the *Richard and Mary*, as well as several of his crew, transferred to the *Duke William*.

An officer from the *Richard and Mary* had returned to the Strait of Canso and contacted transports that had earlier left Port-la-Joie, but had not yet exited the strait. On learning what had happened, Charles Hay created space for the stranded troops on the *Three Sisters* by transferring its passengers to some of the other vessels destined to France. The *Three Sisters* then proceeded to Louisbourg, arriving on November 22. This vessel appears to have subsequently sailed for France, probably with deportees from Île Royale taken aboard at Louisbourg. Some of the troops who had been on the *Richard and Mary* were in bad health and unfit for duty. Eighteen were given leave of absence and sent to Boston. The remainder was immediately put aboard a schooner bound for Halifax, which set out from Louisbourg on November 22. The schooner encountered storms and was almost lost, but succeeded in getting back into Louisbourg on December 8. By then, its passengers were in such a weak and sickly condition that they all had to be brought ashore and hospitalized.

Voyage across the ocean

The remaining eleven transports, having passed through the strait and into Chedabucto Bay unharmed, regrouped before heading across the Atlantic. Because of the delays, provisions aboard the vessels had been depleted more than expected. Most of the vessels had lost anchors and cables and sustained sail damage because of the fierce weather encountered near the Strait of Canso. Consequently, Hay instructed the captains of the vessels to head for the nearest port in England to replenish their larders and obtain other critically needed supplies before going to Saint-Malo, France. The transports varied in size from 183 tons, with a crew of thirteen, to 400 tons, with a standard crew of twenty-eight. Most carried at least six guns and the largest vessel, the *Duke William*, carried ten.

It is a relatively well-known aspect of the deportation from Île Saint-Jean that the *Duke William* and the *Violet* sank as they neared Europe, and lost almost all of their passengers. The circumstances of this tragedy are recounted in Chapter 6. Little has been published, however, about the other transports and their human cargo. A complete picture may never be known, but a great deal more information is available than has previously been reported. It is probable that the eleven vessels attempted to remain in convoy, but that this proved impossible due to rough weather. Three sank or were wrecked partway across the Atlantic. The eight remaining transports reached France. At least three of these, and likely all eight, are known to have stopped in England on the way. Lists of the names of the Acadian deportees who arrived at Saint-Malo also provide the names of the vessels they travelled on, and the dates on which these ships arrived. They also include the names of passengers who died during the trip, the names of those who had to be hospitalized on arrival, and information about

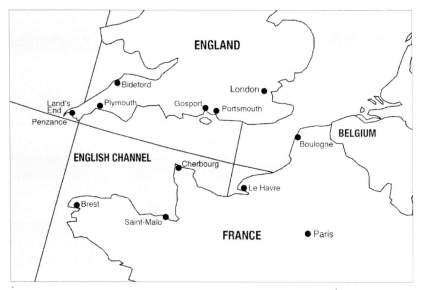

Ports in England and France that played a role in the deportation from Île Saint-Jean

what became (in the short term) of many of the passengers who arrived at Saint-Malo.

Arriving on the other side

The *Tamerlane*, carrying Charles Hay, arrived at Plymouth on about December 16. It had lost all its anchors and cables, and some of its sails before leaving Chedabucto Bay. On January 16 the *Tamerlane* became the first vessel to arrive at Saint-Malo where fifty-four passengers disembarked. This suggests it had spent two to three weeks in Plymouth. The agent, Charles Hay, was once again on board, along with Captain Suttie and fourteen crewmen.

On January 23, the *John and Samuel, Mathias, Patience, Restoration*, and

Most of the transports carrying deportees to France stopped at Plymouth Harbour to replenish their supplies.

Yarmouth unloaded between 665 and 690 passengers at Saint-Malo. Some of these passengers were from the parish of Saint Pierre-du-Nord, and, arguably, the most precious possessions they brought with them were three volumes comprising the parish registers, with entries dating from June 1724 to August 1758. At the beginning of February, the *Mathias* and the *Yarmouth* travelled from Saint-Malo to the Downs, an area in the English Channel off the east Kent coast used by the British navy as a base for warships. These two vessels were unable to pick up any English prisoners at Saint-Malo in exchange for prisoners from Île Saint-Jean because French authorities deemed the latter to be neither soldiers nor navy men, and therefore not prisoners of war. The agreement on the exchange of prisoners applied, at least from the French viewpoint, only to military prisoners. For this reason, it is unlikely that any of the other transports that disembarked passengers in France from Île Saint-Jean were able to take aboard British

Saint-Malo was the intended destination of the transports carrying deportees from Île Saint-Jean; however, only seven of the thirteen vessels reached the port.

prisoners in accordance with Boscawen's instructions.

The *Supply* arrived at the English port of Bideford in County Devon about December 20 with 160 passengers. The vessel had run low on provisions and Admiralty authorities ordered that provisions for five weeks be provided immediately. They further informed local officials that "the ship may not be detained a moment longer than necessary, and as soon as she is victualled it is their Lordships' direction that you hasten her away." Exactly what transpired over the next two months or so is unknown. Provisioning for five weeks seems inconsistent with plans for an immediate departure for France—the distance by sea from Bideford to Saint-Malo is only about 280 nautical miles, or a little over 500 kilometres. In any event it was not until March 9, more than two months later, that the *Supply* reached Saint-Malo, where port authorities reported that 140 passengers disembarked—25 fewer than had embarked at Île Saint-Jean. Evidently, the majority of those who died succumbed between the time the *Supply* reached England and the time of its arrival at Saint-Malo.

About December 23 the *Neptune* arrived at Portsmouth "in great distress, being in want of fresh Provisions and very Sickly." In addition to provisions and other necessities, a French surgeon was put aboard, and within several days of its arrival the vessel sailed for France. However, more gales were encountered and the *Neptune* was blown off course. It managed to take refuge at Boulogne, arriving there on December 26 with 179 passengers. About a dozen passengers had died en route. Some records indicate that the majority of its passengers were from the parish of "Saint-Pierre et Saint-Paul." This is misleading for there was no parish by that name on Île Saint-Jean. There were however, two separate parishes, one named Saint Pierre-du-Nord, that had its church at Havre Saint Pierre, and another named Saint Paul, that had its church at Pointe-Prime. Prior to 1755 a parish named Saint-Pierre et Saint-Paul did exist at Cobequid (near the present Truro, Nova Scotia), and in the early 1750s, some people from that parish, including Father Girard, had relocated to Pointe-Prime in Île Saint-Jean where they founded the parish of Saint Paul. One may conclude, then, that the refugees who ended up at Boulogne were likely from Pointe-Prime, or from the parish of Saint Pierre-du-Nord, or both.

The appendix contains a list of the surnames of refugees who debarked from the transports that reached France.

Chapter 6

Shipwrecks and Sinkings

D URING THE JOURNEY ACROSS THE STORMY ATLANTIC FROM ÎLE Saint-Jean, several of the transports experienced serious difficulties that had tragic consequences. The story of the passengers aboard the *Violet* and the *Duke William*, in particular, is fairly well known. A lengthy and detailed account of the vessels was published in about 1880 in a book entitled *Remarkable Voyages and Shipwrecks*. This account appears to be based on a diary kept by William Nichols, master of the *Duke William*, or possibly a member of his crew. The location of the diary, if indeed it has survived, is unknown. The published account is erroneous in some respects. Within a day or two of reaching land, Nichols sent a letter to the Admiralty office in which he described what had happened on the crossing. While there is much agreement between the letter and the account in the book, there are some discrepancies, particularly with regards to the date the *Duke William* sprung a leak.

A third account of what happened to the *Duke William*, written by a Captain Pile of the *Achilles*, does not differ greatly from the other two, except in indicating that Captain Nichols knew in advance that his vessel's seaworthiness was doubtful. According to Pile, Nichols was pressured into proceeding by "the Government of Nova Scotia." As one historian has noted, the government had nothing to do with the matter, and "Capt. Pile's story as to the condition of the *Duke William* is not warranted by the facts as we have them." Captain Pile's account makes no reference to the *Violet*.

According to *Remarkable Voyages and Shipwrecks*, the *Duke William*, *Violet*, *Yarmouth*, *Neptune*, *John and Samuel*, *Ruby*, and at least one other transport set out on their ocean voyage from Chedabucto Bay as a group on November 25, 1758. Several days later the vessels encountered a storm that dispersed them. Stormy weather continued for a couple of weeks. On December 10 the *Duke William* caught sight of the *Violet*, and on drawing near, discovered that the latter was in major difficulty, taking in water faster than it could be pumped out. By one account, the *Duke William* developed a leak on November 29 and began taking on water, struggling onward with great difficulty for the next two weeks. By another account, it was after the *Violet* was sighted that a heavy sea struck the *Duke William*, and, on December 10 or 11, breached the hull. In any event, according to Admiralty records the *Violet* sank on December 12, and all aboard were lost.

The *Duke William* fought on; passengers helped to bail with tubs as the ship's three pumps struggled constantly. On December 13 the captain and crew recognized that their situation was hopeless, as the ship was by then very low in the water. They lowered the *Duke William*'s cutter and longboat and launched them with much difficulty; however, these small boats could accommodate only a fraction of those on board. According to Nichols, the passengers, resigned to their fate, begged the captain and crew to save themselves. Be that as it may, on December 13 at 4:00 PM Captain Nichols, his first mate, the priest Jacques Girard, four people who had boarded from the *Richard and Mary*, including Captain Moore, and twenty crew from the *Duke William* took their leave in the stricken vessel's longboat, while the second mate and eight crew did so in the cutter. Within a couple of days, those in the longboat sighted the coast of Cornwall and later came ashore at Penzance. The cutter safely reached shore near Land's End.

As it turned out, one other boat was launched from the *Duke William* as well. Just before the vessel went down, four male passengers managed to leave on the ship's jolly boat. They made it safely to Falmouth. The men reported that the *Duke William* went down in calm seas, its decks blowing up with a noise like a clap of thunder. Admiralty records indicate that the vessel sank on December 13.

According to a letter written by Father Girard, all papers, books, and

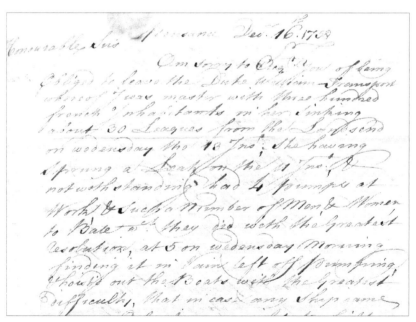

Portion of a letter from Captain William Nichols, master of the ill-fated Duke William, *to the Admiralty.*

other effects that he had taken aboard the *Duke William*, including his parish register, went down with the ship. According to *Remarkable Voyages and Shipwrecks*, 360 perished on the *Duke William* and 400 on the *Violet*. A London newspaper account, apparently based largely on Nichols' letter to the Admiralty, however, states that the *Duke William* and *Violet* each carried 300 French passengers. In his letter dated January 24, 1759, Girard wrote that 300 people were lost when the *Duke William* sank "twenty or thirty leagues from land." On testifying to his superior in 1764 concerning the loss of his parish register, Girard stated that he, along with 366 of his parishioners, had embarked on the ill-fated vessel. In a letter written in 1774, Girard again refers to 300 deaths resulting from the loss of this ship. Some of the variation in the numbers of passengers reportedly lost on these two transports may result from confusing the numbers embarked with the numbers drowned, and not accounting for deaths from disease and illness during passage.

The fate of the *Ruby*

One transport from Île Saint-Jean ran aground as it approached Europe. In his letter of 1774, Girard mentioned that one of the transports was lost on the coast of Spain. He was apparently, somewhat mistakenly, referring to the *Ruby*. This transport, carrying 310 passengers, ran aground in the Azores, which belong to Portugal. It sprang a leak as it passed to the south of the Azores, and Captain William Kelly made for Faial, one of the islands of the Azores group. He was forced, however, to run the *Ruby* onto the rocks of Pico, another island in the group, as the vessel was sinking quickly.

On January 22, 1759, the British government representative at Faial, William Street, wrote British Secretary of State Pitt that "One Hundred & Twenty French & Twenty Three English People were saved." He noted that

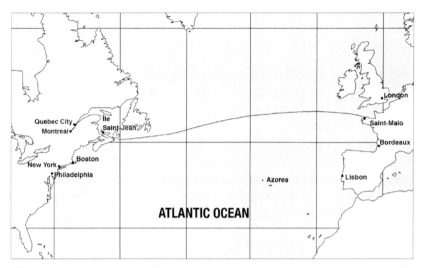

The intended route to Saint-Malo, France, was almost due east. Note that ports along the English Channel are only slightly off route, while the Azores are far to the south.

the *Ruby* was destined for Saint-Malo and emphasized the "ties of honour the English Government was under to maintain & find a passage for the said People," and noted: "I, sincerely regarding the honour of the Nation, have maintained & freighted the Portugese schooner *Santa Catherina* to carry them to Portsmouth, as per Charter party." Admiralty records show that a schooner arrived at Portsmouth on February 4, or slightly earlier, "from the Western Islands, having on board 87 Prisoners from Saint Johns who were cast away in the *Ruby* Transport there."

Admiralty officials had intended to transfer these passengers to the *Three Sisters*, which had reached Portsmouth from Louisbourg, and have them taken with other passengers to the first port that could be reached in France. Instructions concerning this transfer, however, were given too late, and the *Three Sisters* sailed for France on February 4 or 5 without any of the eighty-seven passengers from the *Ruby*. Having discharged its load of prisoners at Havre de Grace (Le Havre), the *Three Sisters* was back in Portsmouth by February 10. Meanwhile, arrangements were made to transport the shipwrecked people of Île Saint-Jean from Portsmouth to France on the *Bird*. This tender departed Portsmouth by February 10 and probably discharged its passengers at Havre de Grace.

It is not clear why only 87 passengers from the *Ruby* were taken on the Portuguese schooner *Santa Catherina* to Portsmouth, if 120 French and 23 English survived. Possibly, the remaining survivors were sent to England, France, or even Portugal on another vessel. It would appear that about 190 of the passengers from the *Ruby* lost their lives aboard the ship as a result of disease, or by drowning off the coast of Pico. Some of those who survived the shipwreck may have died of disease before they could be taken to Portsmouth. Records show that the *Ruby*'s full complement of officers and crew was 27, and a staffing inventory taken in July 1758 indicated an actual number of 26. It seems clear that almost all the crew survived the sinking of the *Ruby*. All of the *Duke William*'s officers and crew managed to save themselves as well. Considering the magnitude of the loss of passengers on both vessels, William Street's remarks about the "honour of the Nation" seem somewhat misplaced.

Chapter 7

Sickness and Other Miseries

THE PROLONGED MISERY OF THE *MARY'S* PASSENGERS IS PARTICU-
LARLY heart-rending—day after day, deaths occurred aboard the
ship. The *Mary's* fate is well-documented. At six hundred tons it was larger
than any of the transports that went to Port-la-Joie (half as large again as
the *Duke William*). The *Mary* took on passengers in Louisbourg, embarking those who had come from Île Saint-Jean on September 4 and who
were not associated with the military or administration. On September 26
Boscawen ordered the *Mary* to receive 540 prisoners and to proceed from
Louisbourg to Saint-Malo.

On November 1 a dispatch was sent from Spithead (a sheltered outer
harbour of Portsmouth) to Admiralty authorities in London, stating that
the *"Mary* Transport, Alexr Donaldson, Master from Louisbourg to St
Maloes, with french prisoners, came to anchor at Mother Bank last night.
The Master informs That he left Louisbourg the 27 Sept. having 560 french

The large transport Mary *stopped at Portsmouth Harbour because of excessive leakage of water into its hull. Many of its passengers died en route.*

prisoners aboard belonging to the Island St Johns." The dispatch went on to say that the *Mary* was very leaky, that her pumps were constantly going, and she was unable to continue her voyage.

"Malignant Distemper"

This was not the only problem experienced by the *Mary*. A large number (perhaps most) of her passengers suffered from "Malignant Distemper" on the voyage from Louisbourg, and many deaths occurred en route. Captain Donaldson buried 250 to 260 passengers at sea, mostly children. The dispatch concluded with the comments "I will suffer none [from the *Mary*] to come on shore at present; And those who are got ashore already, I will take up as soon as they can be found."

Two days later authorities in London ordered the Commissioners for the Sick and Wounded to bring another vessel alongside the *Mary*, and remove "as many of the People (or all of them) as shall be necessary for the Recovery of their Health." Instructions were given to issue prisoners with "Provisions and refreshments." Surgeons were told to provide medical care. A dispatch from Spithead, dated November 12, indicates that the tenders *Bird* and *Desire* were ordered to receive passengers from the *Mary*, by then located at Ryde, a few kilometres from Portsmouth. According to the dispatch, "the Masters have been remiss in following the Directions I gave them upon that head, in so much that, none of the People have been taken on board till this Day." The crews of the tenders had deserted because they were "apprehensive of the Distemper aboard the *Mary*." Having been "reduced to a very great Distress," the passengers had applied to be sent to any part of France. Since the *Mary* was too leaky to proceed to France, authorities in Spithead proposed to Admiralty officials in London that the two tenders take the passengers to France instead "which will be highly acceptable to the poor People, and Convenient to His Majesty's service here."

A surgeon's report of November 12 indicated that he did not believe the illness aboard the ship was contagious. He wrote that the passengers' "Disorders seem to proceed more from the want of the Necessaries of Life, than any other thing." Based on what he had learned from the surgeon, an Admiralty official wrote that the passengers appeared to be starving and were almost naked. In addition, he wrote: "Their having been so much crowded, and breathing consequently foul Air, and lying Dirty, he [the surgeon] thinks to be the occasion of the Loss of such numbers as have already Dyed."

More trouble for the *Mary*'s passengers

Authorities at Spithead told their superiors in London that there was evidence to suggest that Captain Donaldson had not treated the passengers well on the voyage, and had been negligent toward them after arriving in

England. The Admiralty was concerned not just for the passengers of the *Mary*, but also for how the Admiralty would be viewed by France. An official at Spithead wrote: "I would beg leave to submit to their Lordships, how proper it might be, to order them some clothing, especially Linnen, some of the women and Children being Naked; And, likewise, not to confine them to the Common allowance of Provisions, as they are at present extremely extenuated, and will make, at best, but a very poor Figure in their own Country; which May give occasion to make Reflection on the usage they have met with."

The *Mary*'s most sickly passengers were put aboard the *Desire* on November 12, extra provisions were made available to them, and replacement crews provided for both tenders. The following day instructions were issued in London ordering the *Bird* and *Desire* to take the passengers of the *Mary* to the nearest port in France, under a flag of truce, as soon as they were well enough to make the trip. The nearest port in France was Cherbourg. On November 15 the Admiralty decided to place a French surgeon and some medicine aboard each of the tenders.

Two British vessels described by French authorities as packet boats arrived at Cherbourg from Portsmouth in the latter half of November with passengers from Île Saint-Jean and Île Royale. Some or all of these people were probably passengers taken off the *Mary* at Portsmouth. A port official at Cherbourg reported to authorities in Paris that the captain of one of the packet boats set sail for its return to Portsmouth without unloading chests containing the prisoners' personal effects and some silver. Items stolen from the prisoners were found on the harbourmaster's premises at Cherbourg, implicating him in the affair.

Upon his return to Portsmouth, the master of the *Desire* acknowledged having taken "some empty chests" from Cherbourg. The Admiralty removed the master from its service pending further enquiry, and Admiralty officials considering the case thought that his pay should be suspended until the matter was cleared up. The examination report, which was forwarded to London on December 16, 1758, indicated that a port worker at Cherbourg charged with retrieving the chests after the passengers disembarked, broke open some chests, helped himself to what he wanted, and left the chests aboard the ship. The six crewmen of the *Desire* who were examined for the report claimed that they did not discover the remaining chests until the *Desire* was nearing England. At that point the master and crew divided the spoils, which they claimed were table linen and women's clothing worth not more than ten pounds. On November 17 the Admiralty instructed Captain Donaldson to proceed with his vessel under convoy to the British port where the *Mary* would be discharged from Admiralty service. This appears to have been a routine order, not a censure or a disciplinary action.

Acadians in England

A few of Île Saint-Jean's inhabitants who landed in England directly from the Island may have been held there until 1763 when the Seven Years' War ended. The Acadians deported to Virginia in 1755 were ultimately sent to England, where they were held in various towns and cities until 1763. In May of that year, as preparations were made to send these refugees to France, problems emerged for French officials in England concerning who should be considered Acadian. At issue in particular was whether the term Acadian should apply to about forty settlers who had lived in Île Saint-Jean. This might suggest that passengers from one or more unidentified transports reached England in late 1758 or early 1759, and were held there for the next four years. Alternatively, some of the passengers from the *Mary*, under the command of Captain Donaldson, may have remained in England in late 1758. Still another possibility is that some of the survivors of the *Ruby* were not transferred from England to France in early 1759. The Portuguese schooner that conveyed survivors of the wreck of the *Ruby* from the Azores to Portsmouth reportedly brought only 87 prisoners. Since 120 were reported saved in the Azores, some or all of the remaining 33 may have reached England on another vessel, and not been sent to France until 1763.

The most likely explanation, however, for the presence of inhabitants from Île Saint-Jean in England in 1763 is that they were captured at sea by the British during the Seven Years' War. Some of the deportees from Île Saint-Jean are known to have become involved in privateering after they arrived in France, and some may also have served on French warships. If and when captured, they almost certainly would have been detained in England.

Lives lost at sea

In total, seventeen transports were ordered to proceed to Île Saint-Jean from Louisbourg on September 11 and September 18. Residents of Île Saint-Jean embarked thirteen of the vessels and departed Port-la-Joie for France. Only eleven, however, actually left Chedabucto Bay en route to France—and of these, the three largest, the *Duke William*, *Violet*, and *Ruby* were lost. What became of two of the vessels, the *Mary* and the *Scarborough*, ordered to proceed to Port-la-Joie from Louisbourg, is unclear. They are not known to have crossed the Atlantic with deportees from Île Saint-Jean. Most likely at some point they simply returned to Louisbourg from Port-la-Joie.

In addition to the deportees on these transports, other transports heading to Europe also carried prisoners, including members of the garrison and administrative officials and their families from Port-la-Joie, who had been taken to Louisbourg in early September. The civilians who were trans-shipped to France, and the military personnel who were sent to England, appear to have crossed the Atlantic safely. Many of the civilian passengers transshipped on the six hundred-ton *Mary*, though, died en route. Illness and death were commonplace on the transports used to deport inhabitants from Île Saint-Jean and Île Royale to Europe. Among the 1,003 to 1,040 passengers carried on the five transports that arrived at Saint-Malo on January 23, some 335 to 350 died at sea. This represents a mortality rate of 33 percent aboard ship. In some cases whole families died. Many were hospitalized upon arriving in France, and of those, many died in hospital. Others who disembarked died within two or three years of landing in France, presumably as a result of disease.

In addition to contagious diseases, poor living conditions aboard ship took a toll, as seen in the case of the *Mary*. When the five transports arrived at Saint-Malo on January 23, a French official noted that the passengers were suffering from epidemic disease, scarcity of food, and scurvy. When five transports arrived at La Rochelle directly from Louisbourg in late October 1758, doctors determined that the bulk of the passengers were suffering from fevers caused by intestinal worms. It was claimed that the passengers had been reduced to eating spoiled biscuits and wormy salt beef.

Some or many of the inhabitants of Île Saint-Jean were probably not in robust health when Rollo arrived at Port-la-Joie. When the five transports from Louisbourg arrived at La Rochelle, a French official there wrote to authorities in Paris, advising that shiploads of refugees from Île Saint-Jean could be expected to reach France. He also wrote that "for more than eight months these poor people had eaten no bread and that they had existed on shellfish." This must have been an exaggeration—surely not all of the Island's inhabitants had been reduced to such a level. At the same time, it is well documented that famine was the lot of many of the residents of Île Saint-Jean in 1757 and 1758, and that many had "suffered greatly."

Chapter 8

Fate of Some Notable Deportees

IT IS POSSIBLE TO TRACK THE FATE OF SOME OF THE DEPORTED LEADERS and prominent people of Île Saint-Jean, as well as that of their families. Records from La Rochelle concerning the status of refugee families of administrative and military personnel in the upper echelons, as of April 25, 1759, include the name Madame Villejouin, wife of Commandant Villejouin. While he was being detained in England, French authorities at La Rochelle were providing rations to Madame Villejouin, her three daughters, a *negresse domestique*, and two Acadian domestic servants. After Villejouin was repatriated to France sometime prior to July 22, 1759, he was made garrison adjutant at Rochefort, and the following year was appointed inspector of all colonial troops. In 1763 he received his last appointment, that of lieutenant-colonel and governor of the island of Désirade, a tiny speck in the Caribbean which later became part of Guadeloupe.

Island priests: Fathers Cassiet and Biscarat

Lieutenant-Colonel Rollo's correspondence provides clues concerning the fate of the priests Pierre Cassiet and Jean Biscarat, who travelled from the Island to Louisbourg to petition to have the deportation at Port-la-Joie called off. In a letter to Admiral Boscawen, dated October 10, 1758, Rollo noted: "the Priests of St Peter [Biscarat] and St Louis [Cassiet] I sent in the first transports." Presumably Rollo is referring to those that left Île Saint-Jean for Louisbourg on August 31. Father Cassiet reputedly left Port-la-Joie with a number of his parishioners on a transport that carried 166 passengers. He is said to have reached Plymouth, England, three months later, weakened as a result of illness. A family tradition has it that Cassiet and his fellow passengers were detained aboard ship at Plymouth with little food or water for another three months before they were able to proceed to France.

During his deportation Cassiet was presumably transferred at Louisbourg to a transport that had not been to Île Saint-Jean. A priest (referred to as a "missionary") is known to have been aboard one of the packet boats that reached Cherbourg from Portsmouth during the latter half of November. It carried French prisoners who were probably survivors from the *Mary*. It is possible that this priest was Cassiet, in which case he could not have gone to Plymouth or languished in England for three months. If indeed he landed in Plymouth, it must have been on some other transport.

It is also possible that twisted tradition has confused Cassiet with the priest named Le Loutre. Several months after Le Loutre fled the Chignecto area, following the fall of Fort Beauséjour in June 1755, he was captured at sea by the British. He was taken to Plymouth and was held there for three months, reportedly in extremely confined conditions, during which time he was malnourished and poorly treated. In any event, after reaching France, Cassiet made his way to Morlaix in Brittany where he remained for some time while regaining his health. In 1764 he testified that his parish register had been hidden from the British soldiers by burying it in the woods in his Île Saint-Jean parish.

Father Biscarat was less fortunate than Father Cassiet. Many writers have claimed that Biscarat's ship foundered while crossing the Atlantic and that he drowned. This claim is almost certainly erroneous. According to Abbé de L'Isle-Dieu, who oversaw the priests sent to France's North American colonies, Biscarat died about the time that he reached England or soon afterward. It is probable that he fell ill on the voyage, and that he suffered from exhaustion and the effects of inadequate rations aboard ship. He may also have been a passenger on the *Mary*, which came to anchor near Portsmouth at the end of October carrying refugees from Île Saint-Jean. All, or practically all, civilian prisoners who arrived at Louisbourg from Île Saint-Jean in September had been put aboard the *Mary*. It is ironic that the parish registers of Saint Pierre-du-Nord reached France safely, while the parish priest Biscarat did not, and that for the parish of Saint Louis-du-Nord-Est, where Cassiet had been the priest, the reverse was the case.

Other notable deportees

There are clues concerning what happened to other Island notables. Jean-Gabriel Berbudeau, who was sub-delegate on Île Saint-Jean of the *commissaire-ordonnateur* of Île Royale from 1751 to 1758 and also the military surgeon, eventually made it back to France safely. Berbudeau may have been with Villejouin while the latter was held aboard a British vessel in the harbour of Port-la-Joie. In any event, on April 28, 1759, he is said to have landed at La Rochelle with his family, in a large group of refugees. It is also possible that he and his family landed there earlier, since it is known that by that date some members of his family were receiving rations from the government. Berbudeau settled at La Rochelle and carried on a medical practice among the Acadian refugees.

Nicolas Deslongrais, keeper of the King's warehouse at Port-la-Joie, who had no family, debarked at La Rochelle, and by April 28, 1759, had left for Paris. Madame de la Bregeonnière, wife of Île Saint-Jean's *capitaine aide major*, arrived at Saint-Malo with a son and two daughters, aboard the *Queen of Spain* from Louisbourg on November 17. On February 21, 1759, they left for Rochefort. If they reached Rochefort, they must have moved on to La Rochelle since they, together with a *sauvagesse domestique*, are recorded as being there on April 28, 1759. The Sieur de la Bregeonnière, who had been an officer at Port-la-Joie since 1753, seems to have reached France shortly after July 22, 1759, following his detention in England.

Perhaps the most notable deportee was Pierre Douville. He was a son of seafarer François Douville, a prominent resident of Havre Saint-Pierre and one of the first Europeans to have settled on Île Saint-Jean. Pierre Douville, who was thirteen years old when deported to Saint-Malo, transferred with his family in 1763 to Saint-Pierre et Miquelon. He became a mariner and established a trade with New England. He later settled in Rhode Island where he carried on a business from 1770 to 1775. With the outbreak of the American Revolutionary War, Douville became involved in smuggling munitions from France to the rebels via Saint-Pierre et Miquelon, and he

This portrait of Pierre Douville (1745–94) is the only known likeness of a resident who lived on Île Saint-Jean prior to 1759.

joined the American Continental Navy. He served as an officer aboard a number of warships, both French and American, until the end of the war in 1783. Subsequently he moved to Saint-Pierre et Miquelon with his Rhode Island wife and one or two children, and engaged in trading with his own vessel.

In 1792 Douville joined the navy of the French Republic, and in 1794 was given command of the *Impétuex*, a warship of seventy-two cannons. That year his vessel was one of twenty-six French warships that engaged twenty-five British navy vessels off the south coast of Ireland in the Third Battle of Ushant. The French were decisively defeated, the *Impétuex* was badly damaged, and Douville was mortally wounded. He died several days later at Forton Prison in Gosport near Portsmouth.

Well-known fugitives

Many of those residing on Île Saint-Jean were able to escape deportation. Villejouin noted that some settlers went to Miramichi, but returned due to food shortages. They may have been fugitives from Rollo's troops, or they may have left Île Saint-Jean prior to Rollo's arrival, hoping to find better food supplies there. In any event, large numbers fled to Miramichi, the Bay of Chaleur, and Québec without returning. After the capture of Louisbourg, Major General Amherst dispatched Brigadier James Wolfe to Miramichi, the Bay of Chaleur, and Gaspé to capture and deport the inhabitants. Later, one of Wolfe's men, Brigadier James Murray, reported having been at Miramichi on September 15, 1758, where he learned that many Acadian refugees were at a settlement about ten leagues up the Miramichi River, including "some Familys who had fled from the Island of St Johns since the taking of Louisbourg." All were starving. They had sent most of their effects on to Canada and expected to soon go there themselves, according to Murray.

Fugitive inhabitants made their way along rivers and estuaries in small boats to the north shore, where they boarded schooners that took them to such places as Miramichi and the Bay of Chaleur.

A number of prominent people were among the fugitives from Île Saint-Jean. They included members of the Gautier and Bugeau (Bujold) families who had been shipowners and anti-British activists in Acadia before moving to the shores of the Rivière-du-Nord-Est on Île Saint-Jean. In 1758, just prior to Rollo's arrival, both families left Île Saint-Jean and moved to the head of the Bay of Chaleur. From there Nicolas Gautier, among others, provided assistance to displaced Acadians and strove to thwart British military initiatives. Historian Bona Arsenault maintains that "numerous" inhabitants from Île Saint-Jean took advantage of the assistance of Gautier and others to relocate to the Bay of Chaleur region. Some of their names show up in a 1760 census of the region. Parish registers for Sainte-Anne-de-Ristigouche for the years 1756–61 include marriage and death (burial) entries which are said to relate to "several hundred" Acadian refugees from Île Saint-Jean.

Bernard-Sylvestre Dosque, the thirty-one-year-old parish priest from Malpec, fled the Island as well. He reportedly spent the winter of 1758–59 at Miramichi. In 1759 he became the parish priest at Beaumont, Québec, and was pastor of the Cathedral of Québec at the time of his death in 1774. Chevalier Johnstone (James Johnstone), who in 1758 was serving as a soldier in the garrison at Port-la-Joie, escaped to Miramichi. A Scottish Jacobite, he had served as aide-de-camp to Prince Charles in Scotland, and fled to France after the Battle of Culledon. After coming to Louisbourg Johnstone became a lieutenant, and apparently was subsequently posted to Île Saint-Jean. From Miramichi he made his way to Québec, where he served as aide-de-camp to Lévis and later Montcalm. Johnstone is probably the only member of the garrison at Port-la-Joie not taken prisoner. He may have left Port-la-Joie shortly before Rollo and his troops arrived. Alternatively, he may have been allowed to depart after Rollo's arrival, since he is known to have had close family connections to Rollo—Johnstone's sister was the wife of Rollo's brother.

Louise-Marguerite Potier Dubuisson, who died at Restigouche in August 1760 and had come from Île Saint-Jean, also appears to have been among the fugitives. She was a daughter of Robert Potier Dubuisson, who served as the sub-delegate of the intendant of New France on Île Saint-Jean from 1722 until his death in 1744. In 1758 she would have been fifty years old.

Multiple miseries

Only one family was known to have been deported from Nova Scotia in 1755, and then deported from Île Saint-Jean in 1758. The head of this family was Félix LeBlanc, whose father was a first cousin of the Acadian patriot Joseph LeBlanc dit Le Maigre. Félix LeBlanc was very involved in the French cause against the English, and in later life sent a petition to the

British soldiers take a resistant inhabitant into custody while a transport waits nearby.

French king, detailing his service to the State. Following the siege of Fort Beauséjour in 1755, in which Félix played an active role, he and his family were deported to Carolina. They made their way back to the Saint John River the following spring with several other Acadian families. It appears that he soon made his way to Île Saint-Jean, since according to his petition, he was deported aboard the *Neptune*. A daughter of Félix LeBlanc, Marie-Blanche, had the unenviable distinction of being the sole Acadian deported four times by the British—in 1755 from Chignecto; in 1758 from Île Saint-Jean; in 1778 from Saint-Pierre et Miquelon to France; and in 1794 from Saint-Pierre et Miquelon to Boston.

Chapter 9

Immediate Aftermath on Île Saint-Jean

S OME OF THE INHABITANTS OF ÎLE SAINT-JEAN ESCAPED DEPORTATION simply by fleeing into the local woods, and hiding for some months to evade Rollo's soldiers. Though Havre Saint-Pierre was the most populous individual settlement, the majority of the inhabitants of Île Saint-Jean and their dwellings had been distributed along the rivers draining into Hillsborough Bay, as well as around the rim of the bay. The location of the *Hind* and the transports in Port-la-Joie's harbour was thus a very strategic one for rounding up settlers.

Rollo's focus on this part of Île Saint-Jean meant, however, that residents of outlying areas had an opportunity to escape his net. It is likely that some residents of Havre Saint-Pierre and of nearby Tracadie were able to flee. Since the fishery was an important industry in Havre Saint-Pierre, schooners and other craft were available to facilitate escape. Malpec, however, is where most of the evasive activities took place—it received special mention in Rollo's reports to Louisbourg. Tradition has it that some of the inhabitants of the parish went into hiding in the woods to escape deportation.

It is probable that at least some settlers in other areas somewhat remote from Port-la-Joie, such as Bedec (Bedeque), La Traverse (Cape Traverse), Rivière des Blonds (Tryon), and Rivière au Crapeau (Crapaud), as well as remote settlements in what is now Kings County, were also able to evade arrest and deportation. Possibly even a few settlers from areas easily within the reach of Rollo's troops were able to avoid capture by taking to the woods.

Acadian allies, English enemies

From the beginnings of Acadia, the French formed a close bond with the Mi'kmaq and Maliseet people. They actively assisted the French in their struggles with the English in Acadia and around its shores. Mi'kmaq from Île Saint-Jean occasionally participated on the side of the French in raids or military activity on the mainland. From the evidence available, they do not appear to have become involved in thwarting Rollo's troops in any major way, receiving mention in only one of the surviving reports that was sent to Louisbourg. In this report Rollo estimated that there were 150 Natives in the northwestern part of the Island, and he appears to have had some concerns about their presence. He reported that "there hath been a large number of young [Mi'kmaw] men in the Woods plundering their Neighbours, & sending their [French] cattle to the Continent, whether they go themselves I cannot say, but if they stay may prove troublesome Neighbours."

With their hands full rounding up inhabitants of other parts of the Island, Rollo's men appear to have done little, if anything, to deter the Mi'kmaq in their enterprise. It would seem that the Mi'kmaq were active in the parish of Malpec and that their purpose was to help get as many of the French settlers' cattle as possible off to Miramichi and to points on the mainland further north. As well, they killed cattle that could not be saved in this way, thus preventing livestock from falling into British hands.

At the time that Port-la-Joie capitulated, British officials reportedly found a number of human scalps in Villejouin's residence. Admiral Boscawen wrote to British Secretary of State Pitt, stating that the Island had "been an Asylum of all the French Inhabitants of Nova Scotia and have from this Island constantly carried on the inhumane practice of killing the English Inhabitants [of Nova Scotia] for the sake of carry-

The Mi'kmaq on Île Saint-Jean did not actively oppose the Acadian deportation in 1758, but attempted to prevent abandoned livestock from falling into the hands of the British.

ing their scalps to the French who paid them for it, several Scalps being found in the Governors Quarters when Lord Rollo took possession." This charge has been the subject of some controversy, revulsion, and denial. Many authors have noted the claim, and the "several scalps" have by a process of progressive distortion become "a considerable number," and ultimately, a "vast number." Two historians from Prince Edward Island, A. B. Warburton and Sir Andrew Macphail, have totally denied the report, labelling it the "grossest misrepresentation," and a blot on the character of Villejouin, a "generous and humane man," who simply could not have been "a scalp hunter or a scalp buyer." Both authors claim that there is no evidence to support "so foul a charge."

In fact there is ample evidence, both circumstantial and direct, to support the claim that scalps were found in Villejouin's quarters. On occasion Villejouin sent Mi'kmaq to Acadia to pillage and harass the English. It is reliably documented that in the summer of 1756 Villejouin sent seven Mi'kmaq on a mission to Acadia. At Pisiquid (now Windsor, Nova Scotia) they scalped two English people, and returned to Villejouin with the scalps and a prisoner.

Pierre Gautier, an Île Saint-Jean resident and a valued guerilla to French authorities at Louisbourg, did his part to obtain British scalps. During 1757 he made three separate forays from Louisbourg to Halifax to reconnoitre enemy troop size, warship deployments, and other military activities, and to take prisoners as a means of obtaining intelligence. According to French documents, Gautier and his Mi'kmaq collaborators returned from each trip with English scalps. Some of these may have found their way to Port-la-Joie, where Gautier was port captain. Official records show that not only did the most senior officials at Louisbourg pay a bounty for British scalps, but that they advised their superiors in Paris of Gautier's exploits and that Parisian officials responded positively as well.

These dealings involving British scalps were not unusual in eighteenth-century British North America, including Acadia and its coasts. Governor Vaudreuil of Québec reported that in the winter of 1755–56 Natives from Pictou had taken several scalps that they brought to Louisbourg. On another occasion an official at Louisbourg informed the minister in Paris that a detachment of troops, some inhabitants of Île Royale, and some Natives, had "destroyed thirty English from a privateer in the Strait of Canso." Ten scalps were removed and taken to Louisbourg. Acadian settlers living at Ramshag (now Wallace, Nova Scotia) acknowledged in 1755 that they had provided provisions and ammunition to Natives from Île Saint-Jean who had conducted raids on English settlers in Acadia.

Clearly, there were many opportunities for British scalps to make their way to the commandant's residence at Port-la-Joie. The British also paid scalp bounties, both in Nova Scotia and the American colonies to the south.

Generally, their bounties related, not to the scalps of Frenchmen, Canadians, or Acadians, but of Amerindians. In 1756, for example, Governor Charles Lawrence of Nova Scotia issued a proclamation that provided for the payment of a twenty-five-pound bounty for the scalp of each "male Indian."

Avoiding deportation once again

The British authorities based at Louisbourg had every intention of resuming deportation operations on Île Saint-Jean in the spring or early summer of 1759, and rounding up those they had missed taking into custody in 1758. Governor Whitmore reported on June 27, 1759, that he had sent three armed vessels to Île Saint-Jean for this purpose and that they were expected back imminently. He wrote on July 7, 1759, concerning a "whole Parish of the Inhabitants of the Island of St Johns that could not be gott in Time Enough to be sent Home last Fall."

Early in the spring he had chartered a ship to go to Île Saint-Jean, together with two armed sloops, to take soldiers to Fort Amherst to relieve the garrison there and to bring back all the French who remained on Île Saint-Jean. The ship and one sloop returned on June 30 with a message from Captain Johnson, who had been left in command of Fort Amherst by Rollo. Based on Johnson's information, Whitmore informed British Secretary of State Pitt that "all the French were gone off to Canada just before our sloops gott round to that part of the Island." It is more likely that most of the families at Malpec left the Island by late fall of 1758. Their priest, Father Dosque, fled the Island in 1758, and if most of his parishioners had decided to remain on Île Saint-Jean for the winter, it is unlikely he would have abandoned them.

Some of the inhabitants of Île Saint-Jean who escaped Rollo's net by hiding in the woods, whether in the Malpec region or elsewhere, and who spent the winter on the Island, may have left early the following spring.

However, the majority of these probably simply went into hiding again, and thus escaped Whitmore's troops in 1759. When Samuel Holland came to the Island in 1764 to survey it for the British, he noted the presence of a small Acadian population: "These poor people were left on the Island after the surrender of Louisbourg, when the other inhabitants were transported to France, as they lived at a distant place and in the Woods, but surrendered themselves afterwards, and when indulged by some of the Commanding Officers of Fort Amherst to live on their Fishery and Gardening."

Lord Selkirk's diary, written forty-five years after the deportation, indicated that the French on the Island were "descendants of a few fugitives who concealed themselves in the woods at the time that the Acadian Settlers were transported out of the country." This observation was made at a time when some of those who had hidden were still alive to recount the experience. Little reliable information exists concerning how many settlers remained on Île Saint-Jean after Rollo's departure, and after Whitmore's futile efforts in 1759 to take those who were still at large. A report in the fall of 1760 from Fort Amherst to Whitmore stated: "the French on the Island have come in." Six families had located themselves in the vicinity of the fort. The term "come in" meant that they had come to the fort to declare neutrality and, possibly, take an oath of allegiance and/or surrender firearms.

Those who took refuge in the woods, or otherwise managed to evade Rollo's troops while remaining on the Island, must have had a difficult time existing over the next few years. By the winter of 1759–60, if not earlier, Captain John Adlam, then commanding officer at Fort Amherst, was issuing provisions "to support some of the French Familys of this Island, who came in and surrendered themselves, and were in such a miserable Condition that they must otherwise have perished." These and other unplanned distributions of provisions brought the garrison's stores to "a low ebb" and resulted in the supply of butter being totally exhausted.

Although Whitmore spoke of relief being provided for "several distressed French Familys" on Île Saint-Jean, the number supported must have been considerably more than the term "several" would imply. Between May 28, 1760, and July 26, 1761, the provisions distributed to the French on Île Saint-Jean included 10,211 pounds of beef, 935 pounds of pork, and 7,907 pounds of flour, as well as peas, rice, and butter. Deprivation obviously persisted for some time, since in October 1762 the fort commander received an application for provisions from sixteen French families that "must inevitably Starve if they continued on the Island without some assistance."

It has been long claimed that those few inhabitants of Île Saint-Jean who eluded Rollo's troops by hiding in the woods were virtually all from the parish of Malpec, and that it was the remoteness of their forest refuge from Port-la-Joie that enabled them to avoid detection and capture. Over nearly a century, more than a dozen authors have made this claim and asserted that practically all of the Acadians in Prince Edward Island are descendants of settlers from Malpec who hid in the woods in the north-western part of the Island.

This notion has now changed considerably, at least in part as the result of decades of genealogical research into specific Island Acadian families. It is now known that by 1763 a few of those who had fled the Island began to make their way back. The observations of British officials who came to the Island in the 1760s have suggested to some historians that wooded areas besides Malpec may have harboured refugees on Île Saint-Jean during the summer and fall of 1758 and spring of 1759, given the reported distribution of the small population. Also, a few inhabitants may have been deliberately left behind by Rollo on account of their being ill with contagious disease—one writer has claimed that a few were left at Havre Saint-Pierre because they were ill with measles. Conclusions are difficult to draw, however, since those remaining on the Island may well have moved from one area to another between 1759 and 1763. The task of trying to establish how many inhabitants took refuge in the woods on the Island

and where, is further complicated by the return of some refugees who had fled elsewhere.

Deportation from Île Saint-Jean, by the number

How many people were deported from Île Saint-Jean? How many escaped deportation? Indeed, what was the population of the Island at the time of Rollo's arrival? Though these questions have been written about by many historians, only a few have addressed them critically. Since the available evidence is fragmentary and conflicting, the answers have been estimates only, and have varied. In some cases the estimates involve misinterpretation or flawed analysis. During the final years of the French regime on the Island, the population increased rapidly due to the influx from Acadia of transmigrants prior to 1755, and refugees in 1755 and 1756. No good census data are available for the last year or two prior to the deportation.

Despite the lack of good census data, there are several population estimates dating from the late 1750s. "An acco^t of the Inhabitants on the Island of St Johns" sent by Boscawen to Pitt indicated that the number of residents on the Island, exclusive of the 692 sent by Rollo to Louisbourg, was 4,100. The sum of these two numbers, 4,792, is one estimate of the population just before the deportation began. A small portion of this population was comprised of the garrison, and administrative personnel and their families, who were located at Île Saint-Jean. They numbered approximately 100.

Villejouin wrote that 700 people were detained with him in the harbour at Port-la-Joie and that about 4,000 remained to be deported. This suggests a population of 4,700, which may or may not make allowance for inhabitants who had fled the Island. Villejouin's letter was written early in the deportation process, so the number of inhabitants who had fled the Island by that time was probably low. Also, he would not necessarily have been aware of every person who had fled. Villejouin's 700 would have included the 100 or so people comprising the garrison, government officials and staff, and their families. Villejouin was the most senior official on Île Saint-Jean, had resided there for four years, and had struggled with the problems of housing and feeding a rapidly expanding population. It is likely that he had good knowledge of the total number of inhabitants in his jurisdiction—better knowledge than one might expect of others such as Rollo or the Bishop of Québec, who in the autumn of 1757 wrote that the population of Île Saint-Jean was "at least 6,000."

The best estimate (in round numbers) that can be made of the population with the evidence at hand is 4,600, or 4,700 if the garrison, government officials, staff, and their families are included. It is improbable that the population exceeded 5,000, and is almost certain that it was under 5,500. The best estimate of the number of inhabitants deported is 3,100. About 3,000 of the individuals included in this number were not associated with the military or government.

Number of evaders

Historians have made widely varied claims of the number of Île Saint-Jean's inhabitants who managed to escape deportation. As no bases for these claims have been provided, they may simply be guesses. The number of people who evaded Rollo's troops can be approximated by subtracting the estimated number of deportees from estimates of Île Saint-Jean's population in 1758. If the population in 1758 was 4,700, of whom 3,100 were deported, the number of inhabitants who evaded deportation must have been 1,600; however, the possible error in that number is fairly large. If the population were as large as 5,000 and 3,100 were deported, the number of inhabitants who managed to avoid deportation would be 1,900. This number is 19 percent greater than the estimate of 1,600 calculated above.

At least sixteen French families, or roughly 100 people, were living on the Island in the fall of 1762. British surveyor Samuel Holland estimated that thirty families resided on the Island in 1764, and another estimate has 300 Acadians living on the Island that year. Almost certainly the numbers for 1764 would have included Acadians who returned to the Island after the deportation, and perhaps even a few who had come for the first time. From the available evidence, it would seem that not more than 100 to 200 people remained on the Island immediately after mid-1759. If roughly 1,600 evaded deportation, then 1,400 to 1,500 did so by fleeing the Island, while 100 to 200 remained. Table 3 shows probable estimates.

Death and the deportation

A complete and accurate picture of the loss of life resulting from the deportation is unlikely to ever be known, but it is possible to obtain better estimates than have appeared to date. Many authors have only considered the deaths by drowning associated with the loss of the *Duke William* and the *Violet*. Almost certainly some of the *Ruby*'s passengers also drowned.

The number of deaths aboard the transports resulting from illness and

TABLE 3 Population Deported From and Remaining On Île Saint-Jean

Total population at the time of Rollo's arrival (Summer 1758)	4700
General population *4600*	
Military and government *100*	
Total number of residents deported	3100
General population *3000*	
Military and government *100*	
Number who fled Île Saint-Jean	1400–1500
Number remaining on Île Saint-Jean in mid-1759	100–200

disease was undoubtedly even greater than the number of deaths by drowning. The incidence of deaths caused by disease aboard the *Mary*, under Captain Donaldson, was unusually high—about 45 percent of the passengers died. The average rate of mortality at sea aboard the nine vessels that crossed the Atlantic safely, including the *Mary*, was 32 percent. On vessels other than the *Mary*, the rate of death by disease ranged from 10 percent aboard the *Neptune* to an average of 33 percent for the five vessels that reached Saint-Malo together on January 23, 1759. The durations of voyages of the *Duke William* and the *Violet* were at least a month shorter than those of most of the other transports. This likely would have resulted in a lower rate of mortality due to disease aboard these two vessels than the average on the nine transports that safely made land. An average mortality of 25 percent is a reasonable estimate for the *Duke William*, *Violet*, and *Ruby*.

Table 4 presents estimates of the number of passengers aboard the transports immediately after the passenger reallocation took place in Chedabucto Bay, as well as estimates of losses due to death and drowning for each transport.

This analysis suggests that about half of those deported from Île Saint-Jean, or just over 1,500 inhabitants, may have lost their lives before reaching Europe, and that considerably more died of illness and disease than by drowning. The number of deportees who died on the way to Europe was roughly the same as the number who saved themselves by fleeing the Island. These figures do not include those who died in France as a result of sickness contracted during the ocean crossing or during the months immediately following their arrival. Records kept at Saint-Malo indicate that at least 205 died within two to three years of debarking there. This is almost 14 percent of those who disembarked.

It is possible that in the coming years more precise estimates will emerge for: the number of inhabitants in Île Saint-Jean in the summer of 1758; the number which were deported; the number who died from disease and

Continued on page 71

TABLE 4 Estimated Deaths of Deportees from Île Saint-Jean Aboard Ship

Name of vessel	Initial Complement of Passengers[a]	No. of passenger deaths by: Disease	Drowning	Total Deaths
Duke William	388	97 (~25%)	286 (74%)	383
Violet	305	76 (~25%)	229 (75%)	305
Ruby	310	78 (~25%)	112 (36%)	190
Supply	165	25 (15%)	0 (0%)	25
John & Samuel, Mathias, Patience, Restoration and Yarmouth[b]	1020	342 (33%)	0 (0%)	342
Tamerlane[c]	61	6 (10%)	0 (0%)	6
Mary[d]	560	255 (45%)	0 (0%)	255
Neptune	191	12 (12%)	0 (0%)	12
Total	3000	891 (29.7%)	627 (20.9%)	1518

NOTE For the transports that reached France, the numbers for the initial complement of passengers (which totals 1,437), and for deaths by disease, are based on French documents that report the numbers of deportees that debarked in France, as well as the number that died en route. For the *Ruby* it was reported from the Azores that the vessel had carried 310 passengers. This is assumed to be the initial complement, rather than the number aboard when the *Ruby* grounded. The initial complement for all vessels, excepting the *Duke William* and the *Violet*, is therefore 2,307. It is assumed that the difference between 3,000 and 2,307 (693) represents the combined initial complement for the *Duke William* and *Violet*. In Table 4, 693 passengers are allocated to these two transports on a prorated basis according to vessel tonnage. Mortality as a result of disease aboard the three transports that foundered is assumed to be 25 percent. Five inhabitants from Île Saint-Jean who were aboard the *Duke William* are known to have safely reached shore.

[a] Passenger reallocations made in the Strait of Canso are accounted for in this column.
[b] Numbers given in this row are totals for the five vessels.
[c] The number of passengers on the *Tamerlane* is based on lists made by authorities in France who also listed the names of six passengers who died en route. The lists for the *Tamerlane* may be incomplete, since sixty passengers is a low number of a transport of 215 tons.
[d] The *Mary* referred to here is the transport that received passengers from Île Saint-Jean at Louisbourg.

Continued from page 69

drowning while crossing the Atlantic; and the number who escaped deportation. Genealogical research on specific families can provide clues that are useful in filling in the knowledge gaps and in gaining a better overall picture; however, such investigation is complex and painstaking. There are limits as to how far one can go with such research, and it is probable that there will always be a degree of uncertainty attached to numbers such as those presented in Tables 3 and 4.

Chapter 10

Myths Associated with the Deportation

THE EVENTS SURROUNDING THE 1758 DEPORTATION FROM ÎLE SAINT-Jean have been closely linked to, and confused with, events of the larger deportation from Acadia three years earlier. The 1755 deportation may in fact be considered four separate deportations that took place more or less concurrently in Pisiquid, Grand-Pré, Annapolis Royal, and the Chignecto region. Since the 1755 deportation is better known than the later one, it has been easy to conflate the two, and characteristics of the earlier deportation have been erroneously attributed to the deportation of 1758.

Longfellow's *Evangeline*

The incorporation of mythic elements into the story during the last two centuries has added to the problem. Longfellow is not known to have ever set foot in Acadia or Louisiana, yet *Evangeline*, his poetical rendering of the legend of the deportation of 1755, has had enormous influence. The legend was already nearly one hundred years old when it was passed on to him during a dinner conversation with a Protestant clergyman. Longfellow also drew upon information supplied by a priest from France and a lawyer from Nova Scotia when he created his vivid, artistic rendition of Acadian history. Over time, *Evangeline* has been adopted by many Acadians as the incarnation of their idea of the past, a touchstone of historical reality,

and even as an unchallenged repository of historical truth. The personages in the poem have attained the stature of historical beings. At the first of the Acadian conferences, the convention nationale held at Memramcook, New Brunswick, in 1880, the poem was quoted as historical fact.

Although it has contributed immeasurably to Acadian history and identity, Longfellow's poem *Evangeline* contains, not surprisingly, many historical inaccuracies. One myth that owes its existence in no small measure to the poem is that Acadians were deported directly from Acadia to Louisiana. In 1755 Louisiana was still a French colony and the British did not want to strengthen it

Evangeline, a creation of poet Henry Wadsworth Longfellow, shaped the popular view of the Acadian deportation of 1755.

by providing more colonists. Acadian deportees were sent to British colonies along the Atlantic coast from Massachusetts to Georgia, where their evictors assumed or hoped they would be assimilated. The next five years saw a trickle of Acadians reaching Louisiana, but it was not until about a decade after the deportation that appreciable numbers of Acadians arrived there. The majority of those who ended up in Louisiana did so by way of Saint-Domingue (now Haiti) or France. The idea that the Acadians were sent directly to a particular area of Louisiana is also incompatible with the allegation that there was wholesale and deliberate separation of close-knit families—something that would be facilitated by sending loaded transport vessels to a variety of widely separated places—yet this contradiction is frequently overlooked.

Powerful, yet erroneous, images of the deportation from Île Saint-Jean evolved in the late nineteenth and early twentieth centuries and have stubbornly persisted over the years. These images include overcrowded transports unfit for sea and the destruction of homes and livestock by the military. They were largely created by two writers who were also priests, and were derived more from assumption or fertile imagination than from fact. This portrayal of the deportation has been reinforced through repetition, as many authors have uncritically taken their cue from previous accounts. As a result, errors and inaccuracies abound in the historiography of the deportation from Île Saint-Jean. Some are particularly deeply entrenched. The claim that the inhabitants of Île Saint-Jean were thrown into overcrowded, old vessels of doubtful seaworthiness, thereby inviting disaster and death, is one of these. No evidence has ever been presented that the age of these vessels was, on average, greater than that of British or French transports generally, nor is the charge supported by available evidence. An inventory of the state and condition of all transports used by the British in connection with the reduction of Louisbourg was taken in July 1758. It shows that all of the transports sent to Île Saint-Jean were "fit for sea." Of the eight transports (all privately owned) that left Port-la-Joie and reached France safely, four had their contracts renewed by the Admiralty, which continued to use them until 1762 or 1763.

Myth of overcrowding aboard the vessels

Another myth is that the vessels used to transport the inhabitants of Île Saint-Jean were overcrowded. This idea probably originates with the 1755 deportation. In that case, Charles Lawrence, acting governor of Nova Scotia, decided on a policy of two deportees per ton of vessel burden (or carrying capacity), and issued instructions accordingly to the key military officers assisting him with the deportation. At least one of Lawrence's officers acknowledged that he exceeded this limit. The number of passengers on most of the vessels was generally more than two times the vessels' burden, and in some cases was considerably more. The *Ranger*, for example, sailed for Maryland with a passenger count of 263, or 2.9 times its burden. Six transports temporarily put in to Boston where officials deemed them to be "too much crowded."

In the case of the deportation from Île Saint-Jean, the fourteen vessels sent to Port-la-Joie in September to receive 3,540 civilian passengers totalled 3,915 tons burden. This is equivalent to an average of 0.90 passengers per ton. Because many of the inhabitants escaped deportation, the total number of passengers was considerably less than British authorities made provision for. The eleven transports that left Port-la-Joie loaded with deportees in early November carried an estimated 2,440 passengers, equivalent to an average loading of 0.68 passengers per ton. Because the passengers of the *Parnassus* and *Three Sisters* had to be placed aboard sister transports in the Strait of Canso, loadings went up to an average of 0.84 passengers per ton. The five transports that arrived at Saint-Malo on the same day had an average loading of 0.87 passengers per ton when they left Chedabucto Bay. The *Supply*'s loading was also 0.87 while that of the

Neptune was 0.82. The *Mary*, under Captain Donaldson, started out with 0.93 passengers per ton, and the three transports that foundered probably had loadings that were not greater than this figure. If the passenger list for the *Tamerlane* is complete, then this transport was lightly loaded with only 0.28 passengers per ton.

While such ratios represent crowding by the standards of passenger ship travel in the nineteenth century, they are not out of line with the practices of British emigration vessels during most of the second half of the eighteenth century. The eighty-ton *Annabella* and seventy-five-ton *Edinburgh*, which brought Scottish settlers to Prince Edward Island in 1770 and 1771, had passenger to burden ratios of 0.8 and 0.9, respectively. The *Edinburgh*, which took sixty-eight emigrants from Scotland to North Carolina in 1770 had a 0.9 ratio. The ratio of passengers to tonnage on board the two hundred-ton *Hector* when it brought two hundred Scottish emigrants to Pictou, Nova Scotia, in 1773 was 1.0.

Toward the end of the eighteenth century and in the early part of the nineteenth, new regulations placed restrictions on these ratios. Nevertheless, in 1832 the Prince Edward Island-built *Calypso*, which brought 197 emigrants from England to Malpeque Bay, sailed with a 0.74 ratio. Several Island-bound British emigrant ships, which for their time were considered overcrowded, were the *Fortune* in 1791 (1.5 ratio), the *Sarah* in 1801 (1.0 ratio), and the *Dove* in 1801 (1.2 ratio).

The surgeon who examined the ill passengers from Île Saint-Jean aboard the *Mary* in England in 1758 referred to conditions as "crowded." Although conditions on the *Mary* were more crowded than the average for the transports that picked up passengers at Port-la-Joie, they were not more crowded than those experienced by emigrants who came from the British Isles to North America aboard British vessels during the decades immediately after the deportation of 1758. Available data suggest that the loading of the transports at Île Saint-Jean, as planned by British authorities at Louisbourg, conformed to common practices of the time and did not represent overloading. Given that the numbers deported were less than planned, passenger to tonnage ratios were better than anticipated.

Myth of wanton destruction on the Island

The most lurid and deep-seated of the mythic images relating to the deportation from Île Saint-Jean concerns the fate of churches, homes, and other buildings. These images probably originated with events that actually took place in mainland Nova Scotia and along the mainland shores of the Gulf of St Lawrence and Northumberland Strait, but have been attributed to Île Saint-Jean. During the deportation of 1755, the British razed Acadian homes in many places, including Grand-Pré, Pisiquid, Tatamagouche, and in settlements along the rivers emptying into Shepody Bay and Cumberland Basin. Within several months of the fall of Louisbourg in 1758, they torched homes along the Saint John River, and at Miramichi, the Bay of Chaleur, and Gaspé. This was not the result of soldiers acting on a whim. They were following orders from the most senior level of the military command to entirely destroy these settlements. Not only were such instructions given, but a number of documents confirm that they were carried out in most instances.

After the first capitulation of Louisbourg in 1745, the British victors developed plans to deport the inhabitants of Île Saint-Jean to France, and to burn their settlements as well. These plans were not carried out. The only instance that is reliably known of British use of the torch on Île Saint-Jean during the French regime occurred soon after the fall of Louisbourg in 1745. On June 20 of that year a small detachment of New Englanders, sent from Louisbourg, set fire to the home and buildings of Jean Pierre Roma at Three Rivers (near present-day Georgetown). Garrison property at Port-la-Joie was also ravaged, and perhaps burned.

That the British might pillage and burn on Île Saint-Jean in 1758 was not unexpected, since they had done so in 1755 in Acadia. In 1757 the governor of Québec, Vaudreuil, wrote to the Minister in France pleading that frigates be based at Île Saint-Jean; otherwise "the English could very easily pillage and burn the habitations which are rather spread out."

Abbé Casgrain of Québec seems to have been the first historian to portray fiery scenes on Île Saint-Jean in a historical work published in 1894 under the title *Une Seconde Acadie.* He writes of "dwellings being given up to the flames," and of "churches and priests' houses, surrounded by budding villages and vast fields of crops, from which protruded here and there the settlers' homes and outbuildings, sheltering nine or ten thousand head of livestock...of all this richness, nothing remained, absolutely nothing but ashes: fire and sword consumed everything." Casgrain situates this destruction in the four parishes Rollo deported settlers from, as well as in the parish of Malpec where, by Casgrain's own acknowledgement, Rollo's forces did not operate.

For nearly a century other writers have echoed Casgrain's claims. In 1905 Reverend John MacMillan wrote of churches in four parishes being "burned to the ground, and only their smouldering ruins left to mark the place where they had stood." He also elaborated on the idea of wholesale destruction: "Their homes in ruin...their farms laid waste....Of five parishes nothing remains but the blackened ruins. The spire of the village church, bearing high the cross, is no longer to be seen." MacMillan also repeated Casgrain's inconsistency with respect to buildings razed in Malpec. In the 1920s, J.-Henri Blanchard wrote in precisely the same vein as Casgrain and MacMillan, using whole paragraphs taken word for word from Casgrain. More than half a dozen other writers have continued this process until relatively recently, though the florid language was toned down in subsequent accounts.

The treatment of buildings on the Island in 1758 is perhaps best described by people who were there, or were in some way involved. On November 6, 1758, Governor Whitmore reported to British Secretary of State Pitt: "My

In this letter, Governor Whitmore reported that Rollo had not destroyed the houses on Île Saint-Jean.

Lord Rollo reports the Island to be a Rich Soil, a fine Country and well worth being Settled for which Reason He has not Destroyed the Houses." Amherst's instructions to Rollo, in contrast to his instructions to others such as Wolfe and Monckton, included nothing about the destruction of property. Other evidence also indicates that homes, churches, mills, and barns were not burned.

Samuel Holland's survey of Île Saint-Jean, undertaken in 1764 and 1765, records 398 houses, two churches, and nine mills. This seems to be fewer houses than needed for a population of 4,600. The census of 1752 showed an average of 6.04 people per household, and if the same ratio held in 1758 this housing would only accommodate about 2,400 people. The discrepancy may be explained by two factors. First, the influx of Acadians from the mainland between 1752 and 1758 undoubtedly increased household size as refugee families moved in with relatives or others while they struggled to establish themselves. Second, there is reason to believe that Holland's survey party missed, or did not record, some houses, perhaps many.

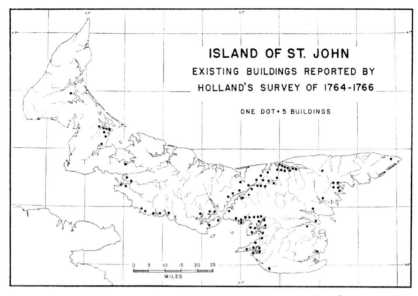

Map indicating the location and number of abandoned homes found on Île Saint-Jean by surveyor Samuel Holland in 1764–65. Courtesy of University of Toronto Press

There is some information on standing structures in Township 13 independent from that provided by Holland, dating only three years after the completion of his survey. Most of the village of Malpec was located in this township. In 1768 surveyor Charles Morris Jr. recorded the existence of the remains of two water-powered mills in this township, both obviously built by the French. A plan of the township produced by Morris also shows what appears to be a wind-powered mill. Holland reported twenty-four houses on Lot 13, but no mills. Holland may have chosen in some instances not to report dilapidated structures, but he did report "a ruin'd mill" in Township 36. Likewise, Holland reports only two churches standing on the whole Island—in Townships 13 and 57. Yet other sources indicate that the French churches in Township 36 (parish of Saint Louis-du-Nord-Est) and another in Township 39 (parish of Saint Pierre-du-Nord) were still standing some years after Holland's survey was completed.

In their enumeration of houses, Holland's survey crews no doubt exercised some discretion concerning what should be classified as a house. Holland observed that of the houses included in the enumeration, "very few...are good for anything and by no means tenantable." By then many of the houses may have become dilapidated as a result of neglect. After leaving the Island following his survey, Holland placed a man and a family in his own house near Port-la-Joie "to preserve it from being destroyed which has been the case with almost all the houses in the Island, as the people from New England and the opposite coast of Nova Scotia carry off boards and burn the rest for the sake of old iron."

Certainly houses in the vicinity of Fort Amherst were pulled down to obtain materials for the fort's construction in 1758. Holland's statement regarding the salvaging activities of Nova Scotians and New England

The Doucet house, originally located at Cymbria and now standing at Rustico, was built in about 1770. Believed to be the oldest existing house on Prince Edward Island, it is probably similar to those that stood on the Island prior to the deportation.

fishermen may have been something of an exaggeration, but even without allowing for omissions in Holland's enumeration and reduction of some houses by decay and salvaging, Holland's survey conclusively indicates that the majority of the houses of the French inhabitants were still standing in 1765. Further, several church buildings are known to have stood until at least the late 1760s. More importantly, there is absolutely no evidence that any structures were burned by Rollo's troops. The Island was not unique in this regard. At Louisbourg in 1758 Major General Amherst ordered his artillery commander to focus his guns as much as possible on the military defences, "that we might not destroy the Houses."

The idea of Amherst and Boscawen ordering the destruction of inhabitants' homes on Île Saint-Jean contributed to the development of a myth of ruthless treatment of Île Saint-Jean deportees by the British. Again, Casgrain seems to have been one of the first historians to put forth this idea. It was picked up by MacMillan, and later by Blanchard, who wrote in 1921 that "a detachment was sent to Île Saint-Jean with orders to deport all the inhabitants and to burn all of their possessions. Every aspect of this cruel order was executed." He wrote in a similar vein in 1927, and at least four other writers repeated this assertion. Forty-three years after first writing on the matter, Blanchard again reinforced the image. This time he wrote that "in his orders to Lord Rollo, General Amherst stated that he would have the settlements in the different parts of the Island absolutely destroyed. It should be done in a quiet way but they must be entirely demolished for the reason that, in the flourishing state this Island is growing to, many years would not have passed before the inhabitants would have been sufficient to have defended it." This misstatement originates from confusion on two counts: Blanchard has confused Rollo with Whitmore, and Île Saint-Jean with Île Royale, where settlements (though not Louisbourg) were burned. The erroneous notion that Rollo was ordered to burn the houses on Île Saint-Jean persists to this day.

Slaughter of livestock

Just as it has been asserted that the inhabitants' homes, barns, and churches were destroyed, it has frequently been claimed that Rollo's soldiers burned or otherwise wantonly destroyed the settlers' livestock. There is no evidence that this is so, although troops did slaughter livestock for their own use, and no doubt to provision transports. Farm animals may also have been taken to Louisbourg to help feed personnel there. To have randomly destroyed livestock would have been at variance with Rollo's desire to preserve farm assets that might be useful for British settlers. Many cattle probably died during the months following the deportation, as a result of exposure to winter weather, or lack of food, or both. When, in 1764, Holland reported that the Island's Acadian families possessed one hundred head of cattle, he may have been referring to remnants of the approximately six thousand that had been on the Island when Rollo arrived. These animals may, though, have been reintroduced from the mainland.

Horses, being hardier than cattle, perhaps fared better. A Scottish visitor to the Island, John MacGregor, wrote in the 1820s of having been "told by an old Acadian Frenchman, that for several years after the conquest of the island, a vast number of horses were running in a wild state about the eastern parts [of the Island]." This would, in general, be consistent with the fate of livestock left behind by farmers deported from Acadia in 1755. In the latter case, cattle, sheep and hogs were taken to victual troops at Halifax and elsewhere, and many of the remaining animals appear, ultimately, to have perished due to the severity of winter, and a lack of food. In both Acadia and Île Saint-Jean, British authorities considered livestock abandoned as a result of the deportations to be forfeited to the Crown.

While a strong case can be made that British officials were ruthless in ordering pillage and destruction in Acadia, one cannot do the same for Île Saint-Jean. It is not just that there is no evidence of pillage and destruction occurring. On the contrary, there is strong evidence that British authorities did not wish to have property on Île Saint-Jean destroyed, and that Rollo's soldiers did not burn buildings or wantonly destroy livestock.

Hiding from the British

Yet another myth is the assertion that those who took refuge in the woods when Rollo came to the Island continued to conceal themselves from the British until the Seven Years' War concluded. A historical account published in 1991 states: "A few Acadians, unwilling to run from the British any longer, hid in the woods of Prince Edward Island for the duration of the Seven Years' War. In 1763, British authorities discovered the existence of approximately thirty families, 'miserably poor, who had taken refuge in the thick of the woods.'" This does not accord with the evidence. Some of those who may have taken to the woods in the summer or fall of 1758 had, as of 1760, requested and received food from the stores at Fort Amherst. By 1762 official correspondence indicates that sixteen French families on Île Saint-Jean were being saved from starvation by British handouts. With this number of French having contact with personnel from Fort Amherst in 1760 (and quite possibly earlier) it is unlikely that others, who may not have needed food relief, would have remained hidden in the woods. Almost certainly word would have gotten around, even to inhabitants of distant Malpec, that it was safe to come out of hiding.

Deportation in perspective

It is important to bear in mind that deportation of the Acadians was not an unparalleled or unprecedented event, as suggested by some writers. Deportations have occurred since Biblical times, if not earlier, and have continued to the present day. The deportation of roughly twelve thousand Acadians from Nova Scotia and Île Saint-Jean pales in comparison to the numbers involved in some other deportations and expulsions, including the Huguenots from France, and the removal of hundreds of thousands of Eastern Europeans to Asia under Stalin.

In the seventeenth and eighteenth centuries, the French government had no qualms about deporting settlers from North American English colonies when hostilities existed between France and England, and when it was deemed to be in the national interest of France. The French carried out deportations of English settlers from St. Kitts in 1666 and Newfoundland in 1696. In 1686 France planned to deport the Dutch and English settlers of Manhattan (but did not succeed), and in 1767 France uprooted more than five hundred Acadians from Saint-Pierre et Miquelon and sent them to France. A modern historian of Newfoundland has observed that "lack of a Longfellow…is part of the reason that the first of the Atlantic deportations [Newfoundland deportation of 1696] remains an historical footnote." It is a sad commentary on the progress of humankind that the vast majority of existing historical works concerning deportations relate to events that took place during the twentieth century.

None of this, of course, diminishes the tragedy of the deportation of the Acadian people at the hands of the British. The event of 1755 in Nova Scotia, particularly as it unfolded at Grand-Pré, will remain the exemplar of Acadian deportation. However, the event of 1758 on Île Saint-Jean (the largest Acadian deportation after 1755) is, in relation to the number of deportees embarked, the deadliest of all the Acadian removals undertaken by the British from 1755 to 1762.

Chapter 11

Retrospective

THE DEPORTATION OF 1755 HAS GENERATED MUCH MORE CONTROVERSY than that of 1758. There are a number of reasons for this. During the former, France and Britain, though engaged in hostile action, were not officially at war, while they were in 1758. Lawrence, the mastermind behind the deportation of 1755, has been condemned by many historians for his inhumanity, though the *Dictionary of Canadian Biography* states that he was "not a cruel man." Lawrence had relatively little influence on the events of 1758; it was Amherst, Boscawen, and Rollo who were responsible for the deportation of that year. Though resolute, they may have had more compassion than Lawrence. It is significant that even after Rollo had been ordered to deport all of Île Saint-Jean's population he still permitted Biscarat and Cassiet to travel to Louisbourg to ask his superiors whether deportation orders might be overturned. In addition, the controversy surrounding the first deportation has to some degree diverted the attention of writers away from the second.

Despair, despondency, and desolation are evident in this depiction of Acadians awaiting deportation. Misery followed the deportees across the ocean.

Although some have alleged the British had a deliberate policy of separating families in the deportation from Acadia, there has been no mention of this happening, even inadvertently, during the deportation from Île Saint-Jean and Île Royale. The deportation from these islands seems to have been handled reasonably humanely, if such a thing is possible. It is true that British miscalculation and delay may have led to more deaths among the deportees than would otherwise have been the case. By the time the main flotilla of transports arrived at Port-la-Joie it was already late in the year—nine weeks after the capitulation of Louisbourg. Had authorities realized earlier the true size of the population on Île Saint-Jean, the delay might have been reduced by a month. The transports would then have crossed the Atlantic earlier in the fall, possibly missing the storms that are common later in the season. Not all of the delays, however, resulted from miscalculation. Bad weather accounted for a delay of one to two weeks during the passage of the fourteen transports from Louisbourg to Port-la-Joie.

The toll of disease aboard the transports carrying inhabitants of Île Saint-Jean was appalling, yet not unprecedented. Death rates of 20 and 30 percent were not uncommon on the transports that took Acadians on comparatively short voyages to the American colonies in 1755. On the *Edward Cornwallis*, destined for South Carolina, slightly more than half the 417 passengers died. Shipboard conditions in the eighteenth century were generally dreadful. Sailors with a British navy squadron that arrived in Halifax on June 28, 1755, were so severely battered by scurvy, typhus, and yellow fever that they could scarcely maneuver their ships into the harbour.

The condition of French soldiers and sailors arriving at Québec City in the 1750s was much the same. In 1757 two thousand French sailors aboard a fleet of twenty-two vessels died of typhus on the passage from Louisbourg to France. The five thousand ill men who landed spread the disease among the civilian population of Brest where, according to one historian, ten thousand inhabitants fell victim to the epidemic.

In the mid-eighteenth century one doctor wrote that "the number of seamen who died in time of war by shipwreck, capture, famine, fire or sword are but inconsiderable in respect to such as are destroyed by the ship diseases and the usual maladies of intemperate climates." Civilian passengers of transoceanic transport vessels faced a risk of death due to disease comparable to that for seamen on military ships. Even in their own communities, French settlers were not immune to serious outbreaks of disease, though Île Saint-Jean appears to have fared better in this respect than Île Royale and Acadia.

That some of the transports from Île Saint-Jean made port in England and in French harbours other than Saint-Malo, was not due to a plot, deception, or treachery. The fierce storms encountered had caused significant damage to the vessels' rigging and hulls, resulting in substantial seawater in-leakage. The adverse weather also caused the transports to take longer than usual to cross the Atlantic. Consequently, provisions, which were already in shorter supply than desirable at the outset of their voyage, had become extremely low during the voyage. Their masters sought English ports where they could have their vessels repaired and obtain provisions more readily than in a country that was at war with Britain. Two vessels ended up at ports that were off the beaten track as a result of stormy weather—the *Supply* at Bideford, before reaching Saint-Malo, and the *Neptune* at Boulogne.

Despite Longfellow's characterization of Acadian life prior to the expulsion as one of peace, bliss, and self-sufficiency, such depictions were far from the truth in Île Saint-Jean during much of the thirty-eight-year period it was a French colony. The inhabitants did establish a new settlement based initially on the fishery, but later largely on agriculture, where they could raise their families, practice their religion under the guidance of their priests, and live as French subjects. At the same time, however, the history of the settlers of Île Saint-Jean prior to the expulsion includes extreme hardship as a result of crop failure, forest fires, and inadequate access to the basic necessities of life. Many of the settlers the British deported were refugees from Acadia who had experienced severe destitution and deprivation from the time of their arrival on Île Saint-Jean. Famine and starvation were frequent occurrences despite desperate pleas to Louisbourg, Québec, and even France itself for supplies.

Settlers had to contend with the political instability of the region, and could never rest assured that Île Saint-Jean would provide the security they sought to live peaceful lives of loyalty to the French king. Indeed, the population of Île Saint-Jean came within a hair of being deported to France in the mid-1740s following the first fall of Louisbourg. At that time some settlers retraced their steps back to Acadia.

The troubles of French settlers on Île Saint-Jean culminated with British occupation and orders for the deportation of the population. The people of Île Saint-Jean, like their kin in Acadia, were unfortunately caught up in a global conflict that lasted close to two decades, and not only affected North America, but also Europe, Africa, and Asia. The Seven Years' War was its culmination. By today's terms the deportation of the inhabitants of Île Saint-Jean was a harsh measure, but it was not at odds with seventeenth- and eighteenth-century thinking, or with the practices of imperial governments and colonial administrations, including the French government and administrative officials in places such as Québec. A more humane approach might have achieved British objectives. If the inhabitants had become loyal subjects of the British crown, posing a threat to no one, their communities might have remained intact. However, many historians have pointed out that it is inappropriate to use twentieth or twenty-first century ethical standards to judge events of two and a half centuries ago.

The Acadian expulsion is a gloomy chapter in the history of Nova Scotia and Prince Edward Island. On the Island, a community comprising five parishes was eradicated. Slightly less than one-third of the Island's 4,700 residents reached France, a little more than one-third lost their lives through drowning and disease on the way to France, and about one-third managed to elude their captors. Most of the latter did so by fleeing the Island, though a few were able to remain.

A new beginning

Fortunately, the deportation is but one chapter of the history of the French in Prince Edward Island. The next chapter was more positive—it included regrouping, re-establishing, and beginning anew. After the Treaty of Paris was signed in 1763, Acadians who had escaped to the mainland began to filter back to Île Saint-Jean, mainly from the Bay of Chaleur and southeastern New Brunswick. Very few Acadians who had been deported to France from the Island returned to what had officially been renamed St. John's Island. A census taken in 1768 shows that the Acadians were clustered at Malpeque Bay, Rustico, St. Peter's Harbour, and Fortune Bay. Acadian families continued to relocate to the Island over the next several decades. By 1798 there were fifty-one Acadian families living on the shore of Malpeque Bay, forty-two at Rustico, twenty-two at Fortune Bay, and two in Township 50.

For close to a century after the deportation of 1758 the Acadians of Prince Edward Island worked at rebuilding an Acadian society. This was hampered by land-tenure problems, which resulted in sizeable groups of Acadians relocating. During these years the Acadians on St. John's Island were largely ignored by the Island government and the Anglo-Protestant population. In spite of this, the Acadians successfully managed to develop their own institutions, preferring to maintain a considerable degree of independence and to hold on to their traditional values. During this era the Acadians, who were mostly farmers and fishers, exhibited little desire to climb the social ladder. Cultural solidarity was apparently more important than personal gain. The stage was set for change when Roman Catholics on the Island were given the right to vote and sit in the legislature in 1830. A turning point was

Stanislas-F. Perry (1823–98) was the first Prince Edward Island Acadian elected to the House of Commons.

reached in 1854 when Stanislas-F. Perry became the first Acadian elected to the legislative assembly of Prince Edward Island.

The period 1860 to 1890 was one of transition for the Island Acadians. Openness to new cultural values, advances in education, increasing involvement in the political arena, and new approaches to agriculture and the fishery each played a role in the Acadians becoming more integrated into the Island's social, economic, and political fabric. Several Acadian national conventions, held from 1880 to 1890, and involving Acadians from all three Maritime Provinces, resulted in the adoption of an Acadian national holiday, flag, and national anthem. These conventions fostered pride, nationalism, and patriotism among Acadians generally, and resulted in a new spirit of alliance and kinship between Island Acadians and their mainland counterparts.

During the twentieth century integration with mainstream Island society has continued. Anglicization, a process that had begun during

The French tricolour with a yellow star in the blue panel was adopted as the Acadian flag at the National Convention held in Miscouche, Prince Edward Island, in 1884.

the transition period of 1860 to 1890, has proceeded. Assimilation and intermarriage with the English-speaking population has accelerated, and the use of the French language has eroded. One may now find Acadian surnames virtually anywhere on the Island. At the same time, a strong Acadian identity has emerged, and a rich and distinctive culture has evolved. Co-operatives, organizations such as the Société Saint-Thomas d'Aquin, and more recently a French school system, have all contributed to these developments. Certain areas of the Island have retained a distinctive Acadian charac-

"Acadian Girl" (circa 1880) by renowned Prince Edward Island artist Robert Harris.

ter, including Rustico, Tignish, and the Evangeline area, of which Abram Village is a focal point.

If any positive element can be discerned from the deportation experience, it is the role that it played in helping to foster determination among its survivors. Acadians responded to the tragedy of deportation by resolving to rebuild and overcome. The few who remained on the Island, together with those who returned, or came to the Island for the first time after 1763, formed the nucleus of a French population which has grown to about thirty-two thousand—23 percent of Islanders claim French ancestry. The British conquerors were unable to quell the Acadian spirit, and their will to triumph over adversity. It is these qualities that have enabled

A group of young dancers exemplify the rich and vibrant Acadian culture on Prince Edward Island.

the Acadians of Prince Edward Island to establish a vibrant community with a rich culture, contributing to the quality of life and economic prosperity on Prince Edward Island.

Appendix

Surnames of deportees from Île Saint-Jean who debarked from the transports that reached France.

The available debarkation lists generally provide the maiden names of married women and widows who debarked. However, it is their husbands' surnames that are recorded here. The name of each vessel is followed by the site of debarkation.

Tamerlane (Saint-Malo)

Aucoin	Dupuis	Prétieux
Benoît	LeBlanc	Rassicot
Blanchard	Maillet	Trahan
Doucet	Michel	
Dugas	Pitre	

Supply (Saint-Malo)

Arseman	Doiron	Longueépée
Benoît	Dugas	Montaury
Billard	Girard	Naquin
Boudrot	Haché	Pitre
Bourg	Haukemer	Poirier
Brault	Hébert	Savary
Charpentier	Guédry	Trahan
Cloccinet	LeJeune	Usé

John & Samuel, Mathias, Patience, Restoration, and *Yarmouth* (Saint-Malo)

Passenger lists for these five vessels were combined by officials in France.

Angot	Chaisson	Girroir
Aucoin	Cosset	Grossin
Babin	Daigle	Guédry
Barriault	David	Guérin
Billeret	Doiron	Guillot
Blanchard	Douville	Haché
Bonnière	Dubosque	Hamel
Bouchard	Dufaux	Hamon
Boudrot	Dugas	Hébert
Bourg	Dumont	Henry
Brault	Duplessis	Herve
Broussard	Du Vivier	Jacquet
Brousse	Forest	Jousseaume
Bugeau	Fouguet	LaBorde
Caissie	Gallais	La Foresterie
Carret	Gautrot	Landry

LeBeouf
LeBert
LeBlanc
LeGendre
LeJeune
LeRoy
Livoie
Manguin
Melançon
Miuse

Morlan
Moyse
Naquin
Ozelet
Patry
Pitre
Porcheven
Potier
Quimine
Rivet

Robichaud
Savary
Segoillot
Staren
Terriot
Talbot
Thibodeau
Valet
Vincent

Neptune (Boulogne)

No original passenger list or debarkation list for the *Neptune* is known to exist. The following list has been reconstructed by Bruno Haffreingue, a resident of France and a descendant of one or more passengers on the *Neptune*.

Aucoin
Benoît
Bonnière
Boudrot
Daigle
Deveau
Doiron

Dugas
Gautrot
Haché
Landry
Lavache
LeBlanc
LePrince

Levron
Melançon
Richard
Rivet
Sauvé
Trahan

Other Vessels (Cherbourg)

People with the following surnames debarked at Cherbourg, were from Île Saint-Jean, and had probably been aboard the *Mary*, subsequently transferring to the *Bird* and the *Desire*.

Aucoin	Fouguet	Richard
Beaudry	Gautrot	Rivet
Blin	Haché	Terriot
Daigle	Montaury	
Doucet	Renault	

At least one member of the Vécot family from Havre Saint-Pierre is known to have arrived in France, but where he debarked and from which vessel is unknown. The list above for debarkations at Cherbourg may be incomplete because French authorities may not have recorded the place of origin for every individual who arrived there. In such cases the individual may have been from Île Saint-Jean or from Île Royale. There are of course no debarkation lists for the *Duke William* and the *Violet*, and no list has been found for the passengers of the *Ruby* who survived the shipwreck of this vessel. Genealogist Stephen A. White of the Centre d'études acadiennes at the Université de Moncton has done some work toward the reconstruction of passenger lists for the *Duke William, Violet,* and *Ruby.*

Further Reading

Arsenault, Bona. *L'Acadie des ancêtres.* Conseil de la vie française en Amérique. Québec: Université Laval, 1955.

—. *History of the Acadians.* Montreal: Leméac, 1978.

—. "Les Acadiens réfugiés à la Baie des Chaleurs, en 1758." *La Société historique acadienne, Les Cahiers,* Vol. 17, No. 3 (1986): 89–93.

Arsenault, Georges. "The Saga of Alexis Doiron." *The Island Magazine,* No. 39 (1996): 12–18.

—. *The Island Acadians.* Charlottetown: Ragweed Press, 1999.

—. "The Settlement of Havre Saint Pierre." *The Island Magazine,* No. 53 (2003): 25–30.

Barrington, George Winslow. *Remarkable Voyages and Shipwrecks.* London: Simpkin, Marshall, Hamilton, Kent and Co., 188?.

Blanchard, J.-Henri. *The Acadians of Prince Edward Island.* Charlotte-town: 1964.

Brebner, John Bartlet. *New England's Outpost: Acadia Before the Conquest of Canada.* New York: Columbia University Press, 1927.

Buckner, Philip A. and John G. Reid, eds. *The Atlantic Region to Confederation: A History.* Toronto: University of Toronto Press, 1994.

Casgrain, H.-R. *Une Seconde Acadie.* Québec: Demers, 1894.

Chiasson, Ansèlme. "Remarkable Voyages and Shipwrecks." *La Société historique acadienne, Les Cahiers,* Vol. II, No. 8 (1968): 286–299.

Clark, Andrew Hill. *Three Centuries and the Island.* Toronto: University of Toronto Press, 1959.

Daigle, Jean, ed. *Acadia of the Maritimes: Thematic Studies From the Beginning to the Present.* Chaire d'études acadiennes, Moncton: Université de Moncton, 1995.

Daigle, Jean and Robert LeBlanc. "Acadian Deportation and Return." *Historical Atlas of Canada, Vol. I, From the Beginning to 1800.* Toronto: University of Toronto Press, 1987.

Doucet, Clive. *Notes from Exile: On Being Acadian.* Toronto: McClelland and Stewart, 1999.

Deseille, Ernest. "Les Canadiens (Acadiens) de l'Île St.-Jean à Boulogne 1758–1764." *La Société historique acadienne, Les Cahiers,* Vol. IV, No. 5 (1972): 200–204.

Faragher, John Mack. *A Great and Noble Scheme: The Tragic Story of the Expulsion of the French Acadians from their American Homeland.* New York: W.W. Norton, 2006.

Fowler, William M. *Empires at War: The Seven Years' War and the Struggle for North America.* Vancouver: Douglas and McIntyre, 2005.

Graham, Dominick. "Charles Lawrence." *Dictionary of Canadian Biography, Vol. III.* Toronto: University of Toronto Press, (1974): 361–366.

Griffiths, N. E. S. *The Acadian Deportation: Deliberate Perfidy or Cruel Necessity?* Toronto: Copp Clark, 1969.

—. *The Acadians: Creation of a People.* Toronto: McGraw-Hill Ryerson, 1973.

—. "The Acadians." *Dictionary of Canadian Biography, Vol. IV.* Toronto: University of Toronto Press, 1979: xvii–xxxi.

—. *The Contexts of Acadian History 1686–1764.* Montreal and Kingston: McGill-Queen's University Press, 1992.

—. *From Migrant to Acadian: A North American Border People, 1604–1755.* Montreal and Kingston: McGill-Queen's University Press, 2005.

Harvey, D. C. *The French Régime in Prince Edward Island.* New Haven: Yale University Press, 1926.

Humphreys, John. "Andrew Rollo." *Dictionary of Canadian Biography, Vol. III.* Toronto: University of Toronto Press, 1974: 565.

Jobb, Dean. *The Acadians: A People's Story of Exile and Triumph.* Mississauga: J. Wiley and Sons, 2005.

Johnston, A. J. B. *Endgame 1758: The Promise, the Glory and the Despair of Louisbourg's Last Decade.* Sydney: Cape Breton University Press, 2007.

Landry, Nicole and Nicole Lang. *Histoire de l'Acadie.* Sillery: Septentrion, 2001.

Lauvrière, Émile. *La Tragèdie d'un peuple: Histoire d'un peuple acadien de ses origines à nos jours.* Paris: Éditions Bossard, 1922.

Lockerby, Earle. "Deportation of the Acadians from Île St.-Jean, 1758." *Acadiensis*, Vol. XXVII, No. 2 (1998): 45–94.

—. "Deportation of the Acadians from Île St.-Jean, 1758." *The Island Magazine*, No. 46 (1999): 17–25.

—. "Colonization of Île Saint-Jean: Charting Today's Evangeline Region." *The Island Magazine*, No. 47 (2000): 20–30.

—. "Discovering Local History Through Church Records of Saint-Pierre-du-Nord, 1724–1758." *La Petite Souvenance*, No. 17 (2003): 19–26.

—. "Deportation of the Acadians from Île St-Jean, 1758." *Interpreting Canada's Past: A Pre-Confederation Reader.* Toronto: Oxford University Press, 2004: 88-93.

—. "Félix LeBlanc—Milicen, Activiste, Aquadient." *La Petite Souvenance*, No. 19 (2005): 14-15.

—. "Deportation of the Acadians from Île St.-Jean, 1758." *People, Places and Times: Readings in Canadian Social History, Vol. 1, Pre-Confederation.* Toronto: Thomson-Nelson, 2007: 168–181.

—. "The Comte de Saint-Pierre and Île Saint-Jean." *The Island Magazine*, No. 61 (2007): 7–14.

—. "Serment d'allégeance, service militaire, déportatations et les

Acadiens: Opinions de France et de Québec aux 17ᵉ et 18ᵉ siècles." *Acadiensis*, Vol. XXXVII, No. 1 (2008).

Macphail, Andrew. "The History of Prince Edward Island." *Canada and its Provinces, Vol. XIII.* Toronto: Constable, 1913: 305–330.

McLennan, John Stewart. *Louisbourg from its Foundation to its Fall 1713– 1758*, 4ᵗʰ ed. Halifax: Book Room, 1979.

Moody, Barry. *The Acadians.* Toronto: Grolier, 1981.

Plank, Geoffrey. *An Unsettled Conquest: The British Campaign Against the Peoples of Acadia.* Philadelphia: University of Pennsylvania, 2000.

Reid, John G. *Six Crucial Decades: Times of Change in the History of the Maritimes.* Halifax: Nimbus Publishing, 1987.

Rieder, Milton P. Jr. and Norma Gaudet. *The Acadians in France, Vol. III, The Archives of the Port of Saint-Servan*, Metairie, LA, 1973. (Contains compilations of deportees arriving in France from Île Saint Jean by name.)

Rodger, Andrew. "Nicolas Gautier." *Dictionary of Canadian Biography, Vol. V.* Toronto: University of Toronto Press, 1983: 338–340.

—. "Gabriel Rousseau de Villejouin." *Dictionary of Canadian Biography, Vol. IV.* Toronto: University of Toronto Press, 1979: 688–689.

—. "Claude-Elizabeth Denys de Bonnaventure." *Dictionary of Canadian Biography, Vol. III.* Toronto: University of Toronto Press, 1974: 175–176.

Stanley, George F. G. *New France: The Last Years (1744-1760).* Toronto: McClelland and Stewart, 1968.

'Tour of Inspection Made by the Sieur de la Roque, Census 1752,' Appendix A, Part 1, pp. 3–172 in *Report Concerning Canadian Archives for the Year 1905, Vol. II*. Ottawa: S. E. Dawson, 1906. (Provides a wealth of information concerning individual households on Île Saint-Jean in 1752.)

Warburton, A. B. *A History of Prince Edward Island*. Saint John: Barnes and Company, 1923.

Image Sources

Acadian Museum of Prince Edward Island: 91

Bibliothèque nationale de France: 13, 14

Brown University Library: 54

Collection Musée acadien de l'Université de Moncton: 27, 56, 87

Confederation Centre Art Gallery: 93

Earle Lockerby: 4, 7, 33, 42, 58

Ganong Brothers: 73

La Voix Acadienne—Jacinthe Laforest: 3, 81, 92, 94

Lewis Parker: 19

Library and Archives Canada: 2, 10, 11, 16, 22, 31

National Archives of the United Kingdom: 21, 25, 79

National Maritime Museum, London: 40

Old-print Limited: 35

Parks Canada: 6

Parks Canada/Fortress of Louisbourg/National Historic Site of Canada: 5
(Image Number 78-R-92-04), 61

Private collection of the Lord Rollo: 12

Steve Bartrick (Antique Prints and Maps): 34, 45

University of Toronto Press: Andrew Hill Clark, *Three Centuries and the
Island*, 1959: 80

Index